"Peter has eliminated many of the complexities of modern Christianity and reintroduced the beauty and simplicity of the gospel. This important and timely message reminds us that Kingdom life is attainable, livable, and doable. Lots of Christian writers tell us where to go, Peter shows us how to get there. This book is rich with refreshing revelation and valuable wisdom."

– Ray Hughes, Selah Ministries

"The Father has one sermon: 'This is my Son.' At the core, the gospel is a person named Jesus. I love Peter Louis and his desire to see others set free by Heaven's song—the gospel."

– Michael Koulianos, Jesus Image

"Before Peter wrote *Back to the Gospel*, he lived it. I've had the honor and privilege of watching the gospel consume the author's life. As his friend and associate, I have seen him embody the message in the pages of this book daily. Peter's message is a tuning fork for the Church today—removing all uncertainty and confusion about why the Gospel is the best news ever shared. I hope every leader, teacher, and pastor will read and proclaim the truths Peter shares."

– Michael F. Miller, Senior Leader, Upper Room Dallas

"Peter Louis loves Jesus. In his book, *Back to the Gospel*, Peter passionately calls the Church back to her roots, where the pure gospel radically transforms lives. He takes readers past the point of simply receiving eternal life, and into the power that is available when we learn to daily stand in the gospel of Jesus Christ. This book has the potential to free the Church from the bondage that holds us back by restoring the purity of our faith, and launching us into the potential we were created for."

- Dr. Kyle Martin, CEO/Founder, Time To Revive

BACK TO THE GOSPEL

REVIVING THE CHURCH THROUGH THE MESSAGE THAT BIRTHED IT

PETER K. LOUIS

Back to the Gospel: Reviving the Church through the Message that Birthed It

Cover Design: Justin Williams

Autumn Williams, Contract Editor

Interior Design: Carson Cheatham, Boldface Why

ISBN: 978-0-9980114-0-0

Printed in the United States of America

To my Father in heaven, may the words in this book reconcile many to you. To Jesus, my King, may the words in this book bring you the reward of your suffering… people who fall deeply in love with you. To Holy Spirit, my Friend, may you quicken the hearts of the readers to experience the power of the gospel.

CONTENTS

ACKNOWLEDGEMENTS

To Kristi Louis — You are my treasure. I love you with all of my heart. You know better than anyone that this book tells the story of our lives and the beauty of the God we love and serve. Thank you for believing in me and loving me with the love of Jesus.

To Justin & Autumn Williams — Justin, thank you for your incredible ability to communicate through art and design. You didn't just create a cover for my book, you created a first impression for my life message, and I couldn't love it more. Autumn, thank you for bringing your tremendous gifts of writing, editing, refining and prayer to this project. I could not have done it without you. You carried this as if it were your own, and I am indebted to you for making this dream in my heart a reality.

To Michael & Lorisa Miller — Few people lay down their lives to see others succeed, but you two have done just that for our family. Thank you for believing in us and putting your time and resources behind your words. This book and message are fruit of the Upper Room and the glorious community you guys have labored to bring about.

To Upper Room Dallas — Keep loving Jesus with all of your hearts. The world needs the flame that you carry in your heart and few communities love Him like you do. I am honored to be in your family and excited to see God's passionate love poured out in our city and throughout the nations. Burn on!

To my parents — The first glimpse into the nature of God, though unknowingly, was being raised by you both. His Spirit, grace and love instructed me as I watched how you both lived out your faith through trials, blessings and unexpected turns. Thank you for showing me what a Christian looks like, and more importantly, showing me what our God looks like. I love you and wouldn't be here today if it weren't for you.

To Drew — As Andrew brought Peter to Christ, so you brought me to the Lord. What can I say? There are friends that stick closer than brothers, but you are my brother that sticks closer than any friends. Thank you for all the wisdom and insight you've given me over the years.

To Abbey — Keep dreaming and keep writing. I look forward to reading your book one day. You are the kindest person I know, and I love you.

To Jim & Janice — Thank you both for welcoming me as your own son and believing in what God has called me to do. I am inspired by how you lead and love your family. I also think I won the lottery marrying your daughter, so thank you for that! I love you both very much!

To Mitchell Orlowsky — You were a great friend and mentor to me. You loved Yeshua like few people I have ever met. You also gave me the most important secret to writing a book, and I could not have written this without that wisdom. Thank you my brother, and I look forward to being with you when I finish my work here!

To Boldface Why — James, you and your team are consummate professionals. Thank you for helping me wade the uncertain waters of publishing and making it a comfortable and virtually seamless process. I look forward to doing many more projects with you and your talented publishing team.

FOREWORD

I'm speechless, quite honestly. I've watched a man pour his heart out into this book, and as his wife, I get the privilege of writing the foreword. Not only have I seen Peter dive deep into this message, not only have I seen him burning with passion from the pulpit, but I have seen him live it. He has become the very gospel that he preaches. I have experienced this gospel through him. There have been many times that I have felt crushed under the weight of condemnation, and when I come to Peter, he says the same thing to me as the Father does. With a smile he says, "Kristi, I don't see anything wrong with you." And that smile...that love has changed everything.

Back to the Gospel is far more than a theology of what the gospel really is. It is an invitation to life. It is an invitation to true freedom. As Paul writes, "The gospel is the power of God for salvation to everyone who believes" (Romans 1:16). In the Church today, we have either relegated the power of God to a thing of the past—something that was manifest when Moses parted the Red Sea or something that came upon the apostles in the early Church—or we have gone to other extremes, believing if we worship long enough and pray hard enough, we will experience this power of God. But it is the gospel that houses within itself all of the power of God, and why? Because, the gospel is the love of God poured out for all of mankind.

There is an urgent call in the Church today, but it is not for more programs, meetings, or worship songs. There is an urgent call for rest, simplicity, and true freedom—the kind of freedom that changes us from the inside out and touches us so profoundly that we cannot help but change the world around us. The gospel is what the Church needs. It sounds crazy, doesn't it? You may say to yourself, "Isn't that the foundation of the Church? Why would I need to get back to it?"

My answer to you is this: If you're like me, you probably had one of those moments, one of those undeniable moments where God revealed His unconditional love so profoundly, and in a moment of childlike faith, you believed. But life has happened since that moment. You may have fallen into sin. Or perhaps you have fallen into trying to be a "good Christian" by putting useless demands on yourself, and quite frankly, you're exhausted.

For both the believer stuck in sin and the believer stuck in a habit of measuring your Christian performance, this book is for you. For the person who is in desperate need of Good News, this book is for you. Or maybe you need fresh faith; your heart longs for a greater experience of love and to know God more intimately. This book will not disappoint you. It is an invitation to unconditional Love in the midst of your mess and also a powerful invitation out of that very mess, not by your efforts but by His thorough, saving work.

So many of us are crying out to the Lord for revival, and I want to make so bold a statement as to say that this is it. As my husband says, "I wake up every morning in revival because I am loved." That, my friends, is the beauty and simplicity of the gospel, and it is the beautiful message of Christ and Him crucified that will bring about the revival we pray for.

My prayer for you is that you don't just read this book and gain knowledge. My prayer for you is that in reading it, you so see His smile that it melts all the shame, sin, and condemnation away in such a powerful way that you become a living expression of Jesus to your family, your friends, and your neighbors. My prayer is simple, really. It is that the love of Christ would change you and that His love inside of you would change the world.

- Kristi Louis

INTRODUCTION
BACK TO THE GOSPEL

"For I am not ashamed of the gospel, for it is the power of God for salvation to everyone who believes...For in it the righteousness of God is revealed."

Romans 1:16-17

It is time for the Church to get back to the gospel. And the gospel quite simply is God's power to save people through Jesus Christ from everything that has plagued us since the fall of man. This ancient message that incited riots and revivals has often been lost and polluted by a "Christian culture" drowning in a sea of sermons and tossed around "by every wind of doctrine, by human cunning" (Eph. 4:14).

Religious traditions and doctrines of men have tampered with this gospel that once produced fiery and passionate world-changers. This tampering with the gospel has produced what we know as "cultural Christianity," those who acknowledge Christ but reflect no real evidence of having been transformed by His life. The beautiful and simple message of salvation offered through Jesus Christ has been diluted through disappointment, failures, and defeat. My heart bleeds with love for the Bride of Christ to be liberated from all that plagues her and to once again become the force of awakening, love, and true revival that our world so desperately needs.

These partial truths lead many to assume that the gospel is merely a promise of life after death. If the gospel you heard only promised you life after death, then you were not taught how to daily stand in the gospel and experience the salvation it offers. That is the entire purpose of this book. My heart is to present the gospel in such a way that the Bride of Christ learns not only how to receive it, but how to stand in it and experience the power of God for salvation in their daily walk with God (1 Cor. 15:1-3). As we get back to the gospel, we will get back to the power of God. And God's power always has a purpose.

In the Old Testament, we find that when God acted in power, it was to save His people Israel. When God parted the Red Sea through Moses, it was a mighty act of deliverance that thwarted the world's superpower with one mighty blow. On Mount Carmel, surrounded by demon worshipers, Elijah offered a simple prayer to the Living God, resulting in the entire nation witnessing the One True God as fire from heaven consumed even the rocks on the mountain. Now that is the power of God! God's power always has a purpose, and it is no different when it comes to the gospel. The power of God is for the salvation of all mankind. These are common terms that elicit an array of responses depending on your religious (or non-religious) background. Even amongst Christians, there is so much confusion over what it means to be "saved."

Since this book is written to instruct believers in how to stand in the gospel it is vital that we have a clear definition of just what the gospel is. I want to articulate this gospel in such a way that reminds us all of God's power and His wonderful ability to save us from the things that plague us all. I will dive deep into this topic of what it means to be "saved" later in the book, but for now, I would like to define the gospel in this way:

> THE GOSPEL IS A COMPLETE AND FINAL SAVING OF MANKIND'S SPIRIT, SOUL, AND BODY FROM SIN, SICKNESS, AND DEATH, EXPERIENCED AND APPREHENDED BY GRACE THROUGH FAITH IN JESUS CHRIST.

This is God's great gospel and the primary subject of the following pages. It is my prayer that as you read these truths and are led back to the gospel, you will be drawn into a deeper love relationship with the One who loved you first. This is what we are created for and what the entire world is groaning and crying out for—that we, the true sons and daughters of God, would be revealed. With this gospel, we no longer have to try to do our best, we simply yield to and trust this man Jesus who has promised to express His life, affections, and love through those who truly belong to Him.

CHAPTER 1

GOD DESIRES INTIMACY

"He went up on the hillside and called those whom He Himself wanted and chose; and they came to Him."

Mark 3:13, AMP

In the following pages, we will examine the why, what, and how of the gospel to bring a fresh perspective and sense of gratitude to those who may have become numb to this Good News. We will explore the heart of God in why He saved humanity instead of choosing to start over again with a different race. Following that, we will discover what God saves us from, what he saves us into, and how we can practically experience and enter into such a great and thorough salvation! For too long we have focused on what God has done instead of being amazed at why He did it. When the gospel becomes a technical conversation about what God did instead of why He did it, we will end up with countless belief systems and cold hearts.

FOR TOO LONG WE HAVE FOCUSED ON WHAT GOD HAS DONE INSTEAD OF BEING AMAZED AT WHY HE DID IT.

So why did God so love the world? God is love. The Apostle John revealed a profound truth to us when he penned these words. God does not just act in loving ways; He is love. His nature and being is the very substance of love, and to know God is to know real love. And for love to truly be love, it requires something or someone to bestow itself upon. I believe this is why God created mankind and why He chose to redeem us through the sacrifice of His Son. Because He is love, God delights to share His heart with mankind. He loves to disclose His affections to us and to romance us (Ps. 25:14, Zeph. 3:17). I often think about the ache in the heart of God as people busily bypass His efforts to demonstrate that He is real and that He lovingly longs to be near to each one of us. God is not only interested in our being "used" by Him to advance His Kingdom; He knows and cares about the seemingly insignificant desires of our hearts. The ways that God expresses His heart toward humanity are countless, but if we acknowledge a few, they will open our eyes and hearts to see more of the innumerable evidences of His great love.

KITCHENAID KINDNESS

A wonderful example of God's kindness and affection was shown to my wife not too long ago. For years she has loved to bake, and for as long as I can remember she has shared a desire with me to own a teal KitchenAid mixer. She loves the color teal, but we could not justify buying a new mixer just because she wanted a different color. The one we received as a gift when we got married was black, and it worked just fine for about 9 years. Then some components started to wear out, and one day it started to break.

The very next day I got a text from a friend asking me if Kristi, my wife, owned a KitchenAid mixer. I told him, "She did, but it started to break yesterday." Well, to our surprise, my friend and his wife spontaneously delivered a brand-new teal KitchenAid mixer to our house later that day. Our friends had no idea this was a long-standing desire of Kristi's heart. In the words of our friend who gave us the mixer, "I just felt compelled by God all week that I needed to give this to you since I never use it and know that you love baking." Needless to say, Kristi cried profusely as she realized that God cares about the little, seemingly insignificant desires of her heart. This is one of many examples of God displaying His affection to us to woo our hearts to His own and to lead us to fall even deeper in love with Him.

We live and move and have our being because God has given us His breath and His spirit. We wake up each morning and take a giant gulp of His kindness; we sleep each night in peace and with plenty of oxygen because God has so graciously allowed us to do so.

Paul writes, "For his invisible attributes, namely, his eternal power and divine nature, have been clearly perceived, ever since the creation of the world, in the things that have been made" (Rom. 1:20). This means that God can be seen and known through what has been created. A sunset can reveal an aspect of the beauty of God, while a mighty mountain displays His steadfast nature. The sun rising each morning reveals His faithfulness. The ocean's tide reveals His relentless, loving pursuit of each of us. His divine nature, which John supremely summed up as love, can be seen, known, and experienced throughout creation if we only have eyes to see.

And therein lies the problem for most of us. The manifestation of His divine love can be obscured from our vision as a result of personal failures, hurtful relationships, and life's disappointments. Perhaps we have agreed with the fallacies whispered to us by the father of lies, Satan, that defy and deny the good and loving nature of our God (James. 1:17). For if the enemy is able to convince us that God's nature is different than it actually is, we find ourselves in a sabotaged relationship in which we never actually know God intimately or, worse, even have the desire to know Him. Without an accurate understanding of how extravagantly God loves us, we will not have an authentic encounter with His saving power resulting in a transformed and abundant life.

My friend Mike struggled to be intimate with God for years because the religious tradition he grew up in taught him that God was angry with him when he sinned and that he would not find his way back into God's good graces and affection unless he felt "sorry" enough for his sin and did a few of the things that God likes, such as going to church, reading his Bible, and sharing his faith with other people. In his mind, God was the cosmic policeman who made sure he was doing the "right things"; otherwise, he would be punished through difficult circumstances or even tragedy. Like it does for so many, his belief about God hindered his ability to truly draw close and know God as a father.

You may bristle at my suggestion that your life experiences or religious upbringing may have conjured up a misrepresented view of God, but I urge you to lay personal history, hurts, theology, and prior religious experience aside. Let us explore afresh this gospel, this God-man who is mighty in love, glorious in beauty, and adventurous in relationship. In my efforts to unfold the greatest mystery of all time, God in us, it is possible that you may discover a God you have never known.

THE PRESENT PURSUIT OF GOD

Because God cannot change, we can reasonably conclude He is still pursuing intimacy with mankind. The beautiful, uninhibited relationship between God and man that was lost in the garden has been restored through Jesus Christ. When Adam and Eve ate of the tree of the knowledge of good and evil, their spirits died, sin entered in, and it became impossible for God and man to continue the perfect fellowship that they once enjoyed.

His pursuit, demonstrated through the passion of Christ, continues to this day. In fact, I would go so far as to say that the reason you are reading this book is not because you are pursuing God but because He has been and is presently pursuing you. You are holding this book because a Divine Love has been hunting you down and seeks to overwhelm you with His patience, kindness, and mercy.

If you are willing to lay aside any predispositions or disappointments you've had in your relationship with God, at least for a moment, I would like to present to you a God of love, who is longing to know you more fully and be known more fully by you. I believe He can make sense of your hurt and heal it all at the same time. I believe He will uniquely display His heart of love and mercy to you, especially in the midst of pain. And most importantly, I believe He will show you His Son Jesus, Who for our sake became sin so that we would become the righteousness of God.

It is the passionate love of God, this longing for intimacy, that I believe is the driving power of the gospel. I am convinced that the gospel is not solely for those who do not yet believe. If we continually yield to His passion and His pursuit to know us, His divine power will carry us all the days of our lives. Perhaps one of the saddest truths of our day is that many believers have become numb to this gospel's power at work in their everyday Christian lives. They can speak the truths we are discussing here, yet with little or no sincere conviction. Their joy and peace are limited as they constantly feel at odds with God, struggling against the effects of sin and the cares of this world. Jesus said, "He who has ears to hear, let him hear" (Matt. 11:15). Oh, how I long for all who have ears to hear this powerful gospel again and again until it is woven into the fabric of everyday life.

This gospel is for all. It's for the lost, of course, but it's also for the ones who are numb, who are tired of trying to live the Christian life in their own strength, and who are tired of struggling with sin and feeling like they constantly fall short of a divine standard of perfection. These are the ones who, in some sense, are the most desperate because they have tasted and seen that the Lord is good but have since been swept away by a torrent of disappointment and failure. Oh, how the gospel is able to save to the uttermost!

THE BOTTOM LINE OF THE GOSPEL

It is often assumed that the ultimate aim of the gospel is to change our eternal address from hell to heaven. This promise of living in eternity with our Creator, free from all the effects of sin and liberated permanently by the Spirit of God, is a magnificent promise indeed. However, I submit that the bottom line of the gospel is union with Christ. If we understand that this union, this inseparable oneness, was the chief aim and desire in the heart of God for sending His Son, then the various aspects and work of Christ in redeeming us to the Father will become more clear.

THE BOTTOM LINE OF THE GOSPEL IS UNION WITH CHRIST.

Paul stresses this point to the church in Ephesus saying, "In him we have redemption through his blood, the forgiveness of our trespasses, according to the riches of His grace, which He lavished upon us, in all wisdom and insight *making known to us the mystery of his will*, according to his purpose, which he set forth in Christ as a plan for the fullness of time, *to unite all things in him, things in heaven and things on earth*" (Eph. 1:7-10, emphasis added). According to Paul, redemption and forgiveness were given to us through an abundance of grace. And this lavish kindness of God was His way of revealing to us the purpose or motive of God behind everything that Christ did. Paul says this mystery, that is now known, is that God wants union, oneness, and intimacy with His people. The heartbeat and rhythm of the gospel is God's desire to be one with us. If we do not start and end with God's all-consuming desire to be intimate with us, His people, then we are missing the entire point. The true and powerful gospel invites us into constant union with God. It is in this union that we will be swept into the abundant and eternal life, beginning even now.

When this reality becomes the foundation of our Christian walk, we will begin to see what God has always intended for the redemption of man. Because we have reduced the gospel to praying a prayer so that we can go to heaven, we have lost sight of its power. The gospel is not just transformative for someone who has never believed; it is, for all time, God's very present help in our time of need. I am overwhelmed by an urgency in this hour to see people restored to the joy of their salvation. It is the same joy that was set before Jesus, compelling Him to endure the cross. You and I were that joy! We always have been and always will be the object of His affection and the delight of His heart. Believing this is foundational to the Christian faith and understanding the power of salvation. Let's press into this sure and steadfast confidence as we remember the Son of God, bloody and beaten, hanging on a cross, madly in love with us. Remember the words of John: "Greater love has no one than this, that someone lay down his life for his friends" (John 15:13).

The death of Jesus is God's great proclamation, once and for all, that even while we were still sinning, while we were crucifying Jesus, He cried out in love, "Father, forgive them, for they know not what they do" (Luke 23:34). This is the love of God. This means that no matter what you have done, what sin you may currently find yourself in, or what sins have been committed against you, there is a love that washes it all as white as snow.

By the grace of God, may we "pay much closer attention to what we have heard, lest we drift away from it" (Heb. 2:1). We believe in the life and ministry of Jesus reconciling humanity back to God but desperately lack passion to see this fundamental truth restored to and celebrated by the Church. There are too many lifeless and indifferent members of the Body of Christ, not because they are not sincere but because the gospel that was preached lacked the power to truly awaken them to God's divine love. This was my story for too long.

CHAPTER 2

SAVED YET THE SAME

"We have learned to live with unholiness and have come to look upon it as the natural and expected thing."

A.W. Tozer

For many years I wondered why I could think about the gospel and all Jesus did on the cross without having any strong emotional response. It was disconcerting that the greatest act of love that the world has ever known did not arouse excitement in me. I grew up in the church, so I was very knowledgeable about what Jesus had done for me and how it was focal and foundational to the Christian faith. Therefore, it bothered me a great deal that this knowledge did not provoke a reciprocal passion in my heart toward the Lord.

For years, I continued to walk by faith, believing that God loved me and that I loved Him, although I did not necessarily sense strong feelings of love. Still, I would try my best to please Him by going to church and sharing my faith with others. As I grew in my knowledge of the Lord and comprehension of the Bible, I had a desire to share my faith with others, but when I did, to my dismay, I was met with the same numb response to the gospel in the hearts of others. I would tell people about God's love for them and what Jesus did on the cross, but it would be met by a cold and passionless acknowledgement of Jesus and His work. They seemed to know God intellectually, but they lacked any evidence of knowing Him intimately.

To this day I know countless people in the church and on the streets who are familiar with the gospel message. They can accurately recite verses in the Bible and explain that Jesus died on a cross, forgiving their sins and securing for them an eternal redemption. Many people can articulate the concept of God's grace and its implications yet never actually live in the freedom it purchases. I found that, like me, many of these people know the Lord personally yet find it hard to be intimate with Him. They struggle with feelings of inadequacy, unbelief, and a fear that somehow they are still at odds with God.

This was very much my story. I "knew" the gospel, yet I had not been transformed by it. I was still stuck in sin habits, living like the world, and no more transformed into the image and likeness of Jesus than someone who has never heard the Good News. More tragically, because of my sinful habits I seemed to be worse off than those who didn't know the gospel because I was plagued by guilt, shame, and condemnation. Although I had put my faith in Jesus as a young boy, I had yet to live in the freedom and joy that was promised to me. Inevitably, I felt responsible for my failure to measure up to a righteous standard of living, and I got trapped in a cycle of disappointment, striving, and a hidden life of sin and shame.

THE FACTS INSTEAD OF THE MAN

I believe this vicious cycle happens as a result of a scheme of the enemy to get us focused on the wrong things. Unfortunately, it has been a massively successful campaign of the enemy. We are in danger of being blinded to the power of the gospel by focusing on our knowledge of the gospel message instead of on the Man Jesus Christ to whom all of the facts point.

This was my story, one that I grew increasingly frustrated with, so I went to God for answers. I asked God why my heart was numb to the gospel, given my sincere understanding and gratitude for what He had done for me. His response shocked and forever changed me: "Knowing what Jesus did for you will not change you until it is coupled with a deep understanding of why He did it."

I began to sit with the Lord and meditate on the cross, often asking Him very simply, "Why did you do it? What was in your heart that compelled you to hang naked on that cross for me?" God was personally inviting me to see, feel, and experience the passion of Jesus that was displayed on the cross. Yes, He died for the sins of the whole world, but He also died for me. I would sit quietly and imagine the pain and agony He endured and the intensity with which Jesus must have loved me for Him to go to the cross. I began to see and believe that the same passion Jesus had for the entire world on Calvary He has very personally for me at every moment of every day.

KNOWING WHAT JESUS DID FOR YOU WILL NOT CHANGE YOU UNTIL IT IS COUPLED WITH A DEEP UNDERSTANDING OF WHY HE DID IT.

For me, the gospel message does not start with my sinfulness and separation from God. It starts with the passionate and determined will of God to be one with me. It was His burning desire for intimacy that compelled Him to die for my sins, wash me in His blood, and fill me with the Holy Spirit. Knowing what Jesus did will have little power to change our lives if it is not coupled with a deep understanding and experience of why He did it.

I long to see my brothers and sisters in Christ set free from sin, shame, and condemnation by the revelation of why Jesus did what He did and the higher purpose in it all. When the Bride of Christ realizes why the Son of God came to earth, she will once again be ignited with passion, love, and zeal for this Man Jesus Christ.

BEFORE THE GARDEN

It is common for those who preach the gospel to begin with the fall of mankind. They tell the story of Adam and Eve's failure in the garden where everything was lost and the relationship between God and man was severed. We must first get people to understand and acknowledge that their sin has separated them from God, right? This has become a major emphasis and the starting point in most gospel presentations. In fact, the common evangelism technique called "The Romans Road" begins with Romans 3:23, which says, "For all have sinned and fall short of the glory of God." The initial focus and primary message in the "good news" message that is commonly shared today is to first convince people that their sin has separated them from God.

But long before there was a garden, there was a triune God in heaven that existed in perfect, marvelous unity and unending love and passion for one another: God the Father, God the Son, and God the Holy Spirit, communing with one another in love (Col. 1:15-17). The honor, affection, and unity that exists in the Godhead cannot be fully understood with our natural minds. Paul tells us that the things freely given to us by God can only be felt, understood, and experienced by the Holy Spirit who has been given to us (1 Cor. 2:12).

When God created mankind, the heavens, the earth, and all that it is in them, He was extending an invitation to all creation to partake of the beauty, passion, and communion that existed within the Godhead for all of eternity past. Adam and Eve were created to have a love affair with Love Himself. Because Adam and Eve were sinless (God's original design of a creature made in His image and likeness), they effortlessly enjoyed perfect fellowship with God. There was nothing inside of Adam or Eve that caused them to shrink back from God in shame or unworthiness. God's original design and the starting place for humanity was perfect union and fellowship with God. This is the same fellowship we were created to have with God. So Jesus came not just to take us out of our sin, but to redeem us—to bring us back to the original fellowship we had with God in the garden.

There is a scene in the movie *War Horse* that illustrates this point quite beautifully. In the movie, a young man buys a horse and trains it to do farm work in order to help his family's struggling farm. The horse becomes the boy's closest friend, and that friendship becomes the boy's way of coping with tragedy as he goes off to war. During the war, the young man loses his horse. Through insurmountable odds, the young man and his horse are reunited through the chaos and confusion of the war. However, at this point the horse had been found by the army and it was their obligation to auction the horse after the war was over. During the bidding war where this young man has to buy back his horse, an older gentleman comes in and makes a bid that cannot be matched by either of the two contenders. The older gentleman was buying this horse for his granddaughter that he lost during the war as a way of holding on to her memory. It becomes apparent that the horse does not want to go with the older man since the relational bond that the young man and this horse had was so strong. The older man recognizes that the horse belongs with the younger man and decides to freely give this horse that he just purchased back to his original owner.

JESUS CAME NOT JUST TO TAKE US OUT OF OUR SIN, BUT TO REDEEM US.

In the same way that this older man legally and rightfully purchased this horse and ended up restoring the horse back to his original owner, so Christ has rightfully and legally purchased sinful man out of their bondage to slavery and placed us back into our original place of fellowship and intimacy with God.

So the gospel does not start with our separation from God through the fall of man; it starts with God's intense love and passionate desire to be in intimate fellowship with us. Understanding this as the foundation and basis of the gospel message will put the entire story in right perspective not only for those we share it with, but also for our own personal engagement with the Lord. When we comprehend that God's original intent in the creation story was to have fellowship and intimacy with us, we can begin to understand why Christ came and died on the cross. He wasn't only trying to rescue us from the devil or from an eternity apart from Him; He came to restore unhindered fellowship and abundant life. This is why He came to earth, died on a cross, and was buried and resurrected. Understanding His loving intent for union with us is crucial if we desire to authentically and transformationally see and experience the power of the gospel.

THE WHY OF THE GOSPEL

I like to say that the "why" of the gospel is the fiery center of the passion and power found within this glorious message. To this day I continue to spend time meditating on the love of God demonstrated at the cross and as I do, I find that my heart grows deeper in love and stronger in passion. Now that we have examined the "why" behind the gospel, we will now look in detail at what we are saved into and what we are saved from. The traditional answer that many will give to this question is that we are saved into an eternity in heaven when we die and we are saved from going to hell. This is what most people think of when they think of the result of believing the gospel.

As you will discover in the following pages, this New Covenant that we are saved into gives us access to a life of joy, strength, peace, love, and overwhelming victory as we face the storms of life. Not only that, but we will discover that we are not just saved from our past mistakes and an eternal separation from God, but also from all shame, our own sinful nature, and even from the presence of sin in our physical bodies that manifests in sickness and disease.

CHAPTER 3

SAVED FROM WHAT?

"For I am not ashamed of the gospel, for it is the power of God for salvation to everyone who believes, to the Jew first and also to the Greek. For in it the righteousness of God is revealed from faith for faith, as it is written, 'The righteous shall live by faith.'"

Romans 1:16-17

I wish to expound on what our salvation has saved us *from* (sin, sickness, death) so that we can see and experience all of *what* He has saved us *to*. In Christian circles, the term "saved" has become a summary category to describe someone who has either put their faith in Jesus or, at some level, identifies with the Christian faith. It is sort of like asking someone if they have insurance; they reply very simply, "Yes, of course." When asking if someone is "saved," there is typically very little emotion involved in their response, and it is not uncommon to find someone who is "saved" still bound in debilitating sin habits.

But the gospel is God's power with a purpose. The purpose of God's power has always been and always will be for the salvation of mankind. The salvation God offers through the gospel is a threefold salvation imparted to us simply through believing. When someone tells me they are saved, I always want to ask, "Saved from what?" Typically, the term "saved" is used to describe someone that has been rescued from an eternity apart from God in hell. They are referring, of course, to the judicial penalty of sin. But Biblically the word "saved" implies so much more. It is through the Biblical definition that I will expound on the threefold salvation God intended for us.

Let's look at the word "salvation" in the original language: The Greek word *sōtēría*, or salvation, speaks of God's rescue, which delivers believers out of destruction and into His safety. The word *sōtēría* literally means to rescue, deliver, save, and to bring health, both physically and morally. *Sōtēría* is so much more than a promise of living in heaven forever. It speaks of a holistic salvation that touches the human life in body, soul and spirit.

Paul writes to the church, "May God Himself, the God of peace, sanctify you through and through. May your whole spirit, soul, and body be kept blameless at the coming of our Lord Jesus Christ" (1 Thess. 5:23).

As we will discover, there are different terms used to describe the salvation of mankind. When God speaks of saving our spirits, the term justification is used. When God speaks of saving our souls, the term sanctification is used. And when God speaks of saving our bodies, the term glorified (or glorification) is used. You will find that these terms and the word salvation are used interchangeably throughout the Scriptures. So this verse implies that each person is made up of a spirit, a soul (our mind, will, and emotions), and a physical body. The *sōtēría* of God promises power to bring the spirit, soul, and body into a place of righteousness, completely saved and removed from all of the effects of the fall of mankind.

If justification is God's righteousness imparted to our spirit, which deals with the penalty of sin (death), and sanctification is God's righteousness imparted to our soul, which deals with the power of sin (law), then glorification is God's righteousness imparted to our bodies that deals with the presence of sin. This is God's triune salvation that does not happen all at once but does in fact save us from every effect of sin in our lives. What a powerful salvation! This *sōtēría* power is available to everyone who believes. Let's delve into exactly how this salvation is to occur.

> THE SOTERIA OF GOD PROMISES POWER TO BRING THE SPIRIT, SOUL, AND BODY INTO A PLACE OF RIGHTEOUSNESS, COMPLETELY SAVED AND REMOVED FROM ALL OF THE EFFECTS OF THE FALL OF MANKIND.

THE RIGHTEOUSNESS OF GOD

Romans 1:17 says, "For in it [the gospel] the righteousness of God is revealed from faith for faith." Through the gospel, we are saved by grace from sin in our spirit, soul, and body by being made righteous. It is received and appropriated by us through an ongoing faith in Jesus Christ. God saves us by making us righteous through and through (Rom. 5:1-2). The only way the devil has access or legal grounds to afflict us is through sin. Death came through sin. (Justification was the first expression of God's saving power but not the last.) Our initiation into the Kingdom of God, eternal life, and covenant union with the Godhead by the Holy Spirit is experienced by first receiving (believing in) the sacrificial work of Christ on the cross (John 3:16). Personally acknowledging and receiving this atoning sacrifice enables God, by the Holy Spirit, to apply the blood of Jesus to our inmost being, making us as clean and pure as the Son Himself.

This work by which the core of our being (our spirit) is made righteous is called justification (Rom. 4:24-25). This saving work of

God is what initiates us into the New Covenant and gives us access, through this intimate relational connection, to experience the other two aspects of salvation, namely sanctification and glorification. So when we say we are saved (past tense), we are acknowledging that God has, in fact, imputed to us the righteousness of Christ to our spirits, and through the sealing of the Holy Spirit, we can be assured that we will live forever with Him.

My brother and sister-in-law have four precious adopted children as well as a beautiful biological daughter. As you can imagine, the moment they officially adopted their first child, it took some time to sink in for both the parents and for the little boy. Though Nicholas had legally become a part of their family, it took some time for both Nick and his parents to fully appreciate the relational connection that had been established through adoption. Nick didn't realize when he was first adopted all of the benefits and blessings that would come into his life just by becoming their son. He didn't understand, because he was a little boy, that he would get to go on ski trips, have four amazing brothers and sisters, receive an education, and enjoy many other blessings just by being adopted into this family. Most importantly he didn't realize that he had been given the greatest blessing of all in two parents that love him unconditionally and call him their own.

All of these blessings and gifts were guaranteed to him the moment he was adopted, but it took several years for him to discover what he had been brought into. This process of Nick discovering who he is to his parents and the privileged place he has been adopted into is akin to our discovery of what it means to be born into the family of God.

So we are not only adopted or born into God's family. We are also "being saved," and one day we "will be saved" permanently as the eternal Kingdom of the Father is established at Christ's return and the presence of sin is eradicated from the world (1 Cor. 15:1-3). This ongoing daily experience of salvation is what we call our "sanctification." It is learning to think and feel according to the new nature that has been imparted to our spirits. That process of discovery, through a relationship with God, awakens us to what it really means to be born into the family of God, with all of the resulting blessing and benefits that come when God becomes our Father.

As we take daily steps of faith in believing that God has indeed made us righteous in our spirits, our thoughts and feelings are renewed by the grace of God, and the image of Christ is further established in our beings. As the nature and image of Christ is formed more fully in the life of a believer, the result is a real salvation and deliverance from the former manner of life that we inherited through our sinful nature. Our expectation of salvation then must include a very real deliverance from sin in our minds, our emotions, and even our behavior. Failure to understand how God has ordained and implemented His salvation has resulted in countless believers—children who are born of God—remaining stuck in sin and with no hope for any real deliverance until they die. By not acknowledging the power of the gospel to truly set us free from sin, we have inadvertently made a savior of death and undermined the very work of the cross that was meant to save us from all unrighteousness during our life here on earth.

THE LIE OF DEFEAT

When I was younger, a spiritual leader told me that men will always struggle with lust and masturbation. It was probably true in his life, and it was apparent that he had never met a man who had been able to live life apart from these common struggles. The problem with this counsel was that it is not in line with the Word of God. What he was teaching served to undermine the freedom that Christ purchased for us. After hearing his perspective, when I was tempted with lustful thoughts and tempted to act on those lusts, knowing it was wrong and desiring to resist, I would hear the voice of that spiritual leader reminding us that men will *always* struggle with these things. I started to believe that true freedom was not possible and that sinful thoughts and behaviors were always going to be a part of my life. Though it sounds reasonable and almost "humble" to acknowledge that we will always struggle with a sinful nature, it actually runs counter to the Word of God:

> *"How can we who died to sin still live in it?" (Rom. 6:2)*
>
> *"For one who has died has been set free from sin." (Rom. 6:7)*
>
> *"For sin will have no dominion over you, since you are not under law but under grace." (Rom. 6:14)*

God does not partially save us. Jesus Christ accomplished a most sufficient work on the cross, and His power is present and available at this moment to all who will believe. To summarize our salvation as only life after death with no promise of freedom in this life is to grossly underestimate and misrepresent the power of God to bring real deliverance and transformation to the life of a believer.

Part of the reason well-meaning church leaders and scholars have concluded that there is no real freedom from sin in this life is because they have allowed their experience to define their understanding of the Scriptures. Because so few, if any, have ever truly been able to experience a thorough deliverance from sinful thoughts and actions, they have concluded that it must not be possible.

We have reduced "salvation" to an after-life experience and left Christians without any hope of overcoming the sins that beset them. But when the Bible speaks of salvation, it stresses that we are genuinely and powerfully saved from an enemy too strong for us to fight in our own strength. The dramatic and complete salvation we have can be compared to the story of the Israelites escaping Egyptian slavery.

> WE HAVE REDUCED "SALVATION" TO AN AFTER-LIFE EXPERIENCE AND LEFT CHRISTIANS WITHOUT ANY HOPE OF OVERCOMING THE SINS THAT BESET THEM.

COMPLETE AND THOROUGH SALVATION

For 400 years the people of God (Israel) worked as slaves under Pharaoh, the leader of Egypt. They worked tirelessly making bricks, though their taskmasters treated them cruelly. They cried out to God to save them and God raised up a leader among them named Moses who would deliver Israel from the generations of bondage and discrimination they had endured. Now let us observe very closely the salvation God performed for Israel through His servant Moses.

God sends Moses to Israel's enemy to demand, "Let my people go." Pharaoh denies God's command and as a result suffers ten different plagues. The final plague "breaks the Pharaoh's back" and forces him to let the people of Israel go.

The people follow Moses out of Egypt (with all sorts of booty) and end up between a large body of water (the Red Sea), a mountain, and the largest, most formidable army on the earth at the time. Just when they think their salvation has come, they reach a place of certain death. Not knowing what to do, Moses cries out to God! God rebukes Moses and says: "Why do you cry out to me? Tell the Israelites to go forward. Lift up your staff, and stretch out your hand over the sea and divide it, that the people of Israel may go through the sea on dry ground" (Ex. 14:15-16).

Again, God uses Moses to bring about a mighty and thorough deliverance for the people of Israel. When Moses lifts up his staff, the waters begin to part, and Israel passes through the bottom of the sea on dry ground to reach safety on the other side. Pharaoh pursues Israel with his entire army. Once they are all in perfect position at the bottom of the sea, God consumes the entire Egyptian army by letting the Red Sea fall upon them, not leaving one survivor. In a moment, 400 years of slavery and oppression are consumed by one mighty act of God. Now that is salvation!

Let me bring this story back to the gospel and what Christ has done so we can begin to see just how marvelous our salvation truly is. Instead of choosing an earthly vessel like Moses, God chose His own son, Jesus Christ, to be the deliverer. And in our story, Egypt is not the problem enslaving us, but the sinful state we inherited through Adam (Rom. 5:12). The condition of sin and death in the human heart is what enslaves us. But God did not leave us without a remedy. Jesus Christ came into the earth to give His life as a ransom for many. Instead of leading us through a Red Sea, He leads us to His grave, a place of deepest darkness. Just like when Israel was stuck between their enslaving enemy and the deadly sea, so we were stuck between our sinful state and the grave.

This is the victory that we have been reborn into, and it is a thorough and complete salvation. He did not merely rinse us in His blood or settle our record of debt, but by the cross He destroyed sin, sickness, and death by becoming sin and death so that we could forever be liberated from the captivity of sin and fully become the righteousness of God. This transaction is so powerful and that the Bible uses language like being "born again" and "partakers of divine nature" (1 Pet. 1:3, 2 Pet. 1:4).

SAVED TO HIS RIGHTEOUSNESS

We must understand that the *sōtēría* gospel delivers us emphatically and permanently from the penalty of sin which is the death of our spirit (Rom. 6:23) and the power of sin over our soul which is the law (1 Cor. 15:56). The presence of sin in the world will only fully be dealt with when Christ returns and places all of His enemies under His feet.

Likewise, the *sōtēría* gospel saves us into holiness, joy, peace, and power in this life on earth. This is why the commonly used phrase "we're only human" is unnatural for a Christian to say. We use this phrase to identify with the effects of the fall of man on our spirits and souls instead of identifying with Jesus and the divine impartation of His Spirit. If you identify yourself as a Christian, then you should also acknowledge that the cross of Christ, His death, burial, resurrection, ascension, and the promise of the Holy Spirit has delivered you out of the realm of sin, sickness, and death and into the Kingdom of heaven, where righteousness, peace, and joy are your new normal.

Since God is able, through the power of the gospel, to make our spirits and souls just as righteous as Christ, by the sealing of the Holy Spirit, it becomes our inheritance to live in a constant state of feeling righteous, peaceful, and joyful. This is the very atmosphere of heaven, where we are now citizens. The Holy Spirit brings this truth to light in the lives of every born-again believer, but it is imperative to believe by grace through faith (Eph. 2:8), in order to fully experience this salvation in our spirit, soul, and body.

Like I said before, God's power always has a purpose. God's purpose in saving us in such a powerful way from the fall of man was *so that* we could be intimate with Him. I realize it may sound like I am splitting hairs here, but it is crucial to understand the intention of the gospel in this way. The gospel is the power of God to bring salvation (body, soul, and spirit) to all who believe. The purpose of bringing salvation is to establish us in a new covenant with God in order to experience and enjoy an intimate relationship with Him that could not be possible outside of the *sōtēría* salvation I have described. It is in this new covenant relationship that we experience and grow up into the fullness of this salvation.

When someone truly receives the righteousness of God in their spirit by faith, they are convinced there is nothing in their own spirit that could ever separate them from the love of God that is in Christ. They are confident in their relationship with God because they have received His righteousness in their inmost being. His righteousness in our spirits is not merely a positional righteousness, as some will try to argue, but it is an actual righteousness imparted into our spirits by the grace of Jesus Christ. This means through the gospel, by the power of God, we genuinely and literally become the righteousness of God.

CHAPTER 4

THE NEW COVENANT

For I will be merciful toward their iniquities, and I will remember their sins no more. In speaking of a new covenant, he makes the first one obsolete. And what is becoming obsolete and growing old is ready to vanish away."

Hebrews 8:10-13

We know that Israel was saved from their enemies and made distinct from other nations because of their covenant relationship with God. This covenant is now known as the Old Covenant because through Jesus Christ, a newer and more permanent covenant was introduced, as prophesied in Jeremiah 31:31. Understanding the strength and glory of this New Covenant (and the new way of relating to God through it) will help us get back to the gospel so that we experience the power of what has been promised. This New Covenant changes how we relate to God and bestows upon us blessings that are too many to number.

I want to address the concept of covenant, as I believe it shows the foundational power and perpetual joy and hope available to us in our relationship with God. To me, "covenant" is a fancy way of describing the relationship that God designed where both parties agree to wholeheartedly give themselves to one another. And it is through this New Covenant that we experience and enjoy salvation. Not only does God save us so that we can enter into this covenant, but it is through the intimacy and nearness that the covenant provides that we experience the fullness of salvation. When someone hears the Good News and puts his or her faith in Jesus Christ by acknowledging Him as Lord, that person is born again and is immediately justified by that faith.

This is how we enter into the New Covenant with God, by faith in the work of Jesus Christ on the cross. From this foundation of intimacy and righteousness, we can experience the sanctifying work of the Holy Spirit that redeems and restores the image of God that was marred and tainted by the fall of man. We will further explore the ways in which God saves us, but for now it is important to understand the New Covenant that we are born into and the privileges and blessings that are bestowed to us.

I have found that there is some confusion in the Body of Christ when we start talking about the Old and New Covenants as it relates to the Old and New Testaments. Paul clarifies this to his young protégé Timothy:

> *"All Scripture is breathed out by God and profitable for teaching, for reproof, for correction, and for training in righteousness, that the man of God may be complete, equipped for every good work." (2 Tim. 3:16-17)*

When this was written, the New Testament had not yet been written or canonized, so the Scripture that Timothy is referring to is the Law and the Prophets (Old Testament). This means that the Old Testament is profitable to every believer for teaching, reproving, and training us in understanding the righteousness that has now been freely given to us through Jesus. However, within the Old Testament, we read about a covenant that we know is an outdated way of relating to God, no longer applicable to us since Christ has come. In speaking of the Old Covenant, the Bible says, "And what is becoming obsolete and growing old is ready to vanish away" (Heb. 8:13). This means that the way the people of Israel related to God in the Old Testament, through the law, has become obsolete because a better relationship has been introduced through the God-man Jesus Christ.

OLD COVENANT - GOD AS A HUSBAND

A few years back I was teaching a ministry class, and a young man asked me, "What is the difference between the Old and the New Covenants?" To this complex question I immediately had a response in my spirit, which made it obvious to me that it came straight from the Lord and not my own intellect.

I told this young man that the Old Covenant is likened to the relationship between a husband and wife. God made a covenant with Abraham that carried on through his children: Isaac; and Jacob, who became Israel. This covenant was a type of marriage covenant, as God Himself described in Jeremiah:

> *"Behold, the days are coming, declares the Lord, when I will make a new covenant with the house of Israel and the house of Judah, not like the covenant that I made with their fathers on the day when I took them by the hand to bring them out of the land of Egypt, my covenant that they broke, though I was their husband, declares the Lord." (Jer. 31:31-32)*

God identified with Israel as their husband and they were His bride. But because of their sinful nature, they were led astray, and because of their unfaithfulness, they broke the covenant that God had made with them. The problem with the Old Covenant was the possibility of it being broken because it was modeled after a marriage. We know that even though God's design and perfect will is that any man and woman who enter into covenant with one another through marriage would never divorce, the possibility is still there. Just as marriage can be broken by unfaithfulness, so too the Old Covenant could be broken through Israel's unfaithfulness. It is possible for a man and woman to be separated through divorce, and it is in this possibility that we see the weakness and imperfection of this Old Covenant. In his letter to the Corinthians, the apostle Paul writes:

> *"Now if the ministry of death, carved in letters on stone, came with such glory that the Israelites could not gaze at Moses' face because of its glory, which was being brought to an end, will not the ministry of the Spirit have even more glory? For if there was glory in the ministry of condemnation, the ministry of righteousness must far exceed it in glory. Indeed, in this case, what once had glory has come to have no glory at all, because of the glory that surpasses it. For if what was being brought to an end came with glory, much more will what is permanent have glory." (2 Cor. 3:7-11)*

Although the Old Covenant was a ministry of death and condemnation because it came through the law, it also came with such a glory that when Moses received it on the mountain, his face shone so brightly that it was hard for people to look at him. How much more glorious is this New Covenant of which we now partake, a permanent ministry of righteousness through the Spirit?

Now, before I move on to describe the nature of the New Covenant, I want to say something of the Old. Before the New was introduced, this Old Covenant was the highest revelation of God that existed. Nowhere on earth could you find a people who were identified as the beloved bride of the Creator Himself (Jer. 32:38). This was a glorious covenant, which is why we see so many signs and wonders performed on behalf of God's chosen people Israel. God went to great lengths to love Israel, to save the Jewish people, and to bestow His love and favor upon them. Even now God's love for His people and the nation of Israel has not ceased and will never cease!

NEW COVENANT - GOD AS A FATHER

To pick up the story with the young man in the ministry class I taught, I began to explain to him how the Old Covenant was like a marriage relationship, but the New Covenant is like the relationship between a father and his child. It says in the Gospel of John, "But to all who did receive Him, who believed in His name, He gave the right to become children of God, who were born, not of blood nor of the will of the flesh nor of the will of man, but of God" (John 1:12-13).

Those who have entered into this New Covenant with God have been born into a familial relationship that is so much deeper and stronger than the Old Covenant that it will bring us to our knees in adoration and praise if we truly see it! We have now been born of God and this new birth and New Covenant cannot and will not ever be broken.

The example of my daughter, Faith, can help explain this profound mystery in human terms. Faith is literally one flesh of my wife, Kristi, and me. She was knit together with our genetics and chromosomes, born from our bloodline and in our likeness. And now, as my daughter, there is nothing she could ever do that could break that biological and relational bond we share. She could sin every day for the rest of her life, yet that would still not alter the fact that I am her father. She could do well all the days of her life, and that also would not affect the fundamental relational connection she has with me as my daughter. She is permanently a part of me. It is a physical and literal impossibility for her or I to ever destroy or break the connection we have with one another.

This is the strength of the New Covenant that we now have with God. Ephesians 5:32 says, "This mystery is profound, and I am saying that it refers to Christ and the church." As one flesh, we have now been joined together with Jesus, by the Holy Spirit, through His death, burial, and resurrection. When we were crucified with Christ, we were then resurrected and born again into this New Covenant. We become not one in spirit only, but one flesh. And this union, this type of oneness, is what gives this New Covenant such a greater glory. Jeremiah 31:33-34 describes the New Covenant in this way:

> *"For this is the covenant that I will make with the house of Israel after those days, declares the Lord: I will put my law within them, and I will write it on their hearts. And I will be their God, and they shall be my people. And no longer shall each one teach his neighbor and each his brother, saying, 'Know the Lord,' for they shall all know me, from the least of them to the greatest, declares the Lord. For I will forgive their iniquity, and I will remember their sin no more."*

The law was the method designed for humanity to have a right relationship with a righteous and holy God. But now, instead of us being governed by external laws, though they were spiritual and good, we now have the laws (or righteousness) of God written on our brand-new hearts. He has made us His righteousness, a new creation, according to the promise in 2 Corinthians 5:17. It is because of this New Covenant that we who are in Christ can no longer identify with passages like Jeremiah 17:9, which says, "The heart is deceitful above all things, and desperately sick; who can understand it?"

God did not make our new hearts deceitful and desperately sick. He made us one with Him, like Him, bearing His image! This being "born again" is considered a finished work in heaven that is being manifest in us through the Holy Spirit. Now that we have been born of God, the relationship we have with God is like that of a child to a Father. It is permanent, unending, and unchanging. Your confidence in salvation no longer stands solely in the theology or doctrine you believe, but the righteousness you have become in Him.

If knowledge alone is your foundation, your whole life and faith will be shaken when painful and confusing experiences contradict and challenge what you believe. Your confidence must stem from the intimate New Covenant that you have entered into with God and, more astounding, that He has entered into with you. When you surrender to and daily abide in this covenant with God, you give yourself to Him as He has given Himself to you. It is so much more than a new set of beliefs and values. It is a life-altering encounter that spins you into an eternally transforming relational journey with One who is perfect at relationship. It is an exchange - His thoughts, His attributes, His dreams, His creativity, His power are given to you. You abide in Him, and He abides in you. You become one with God.

In this type of covenant, your faith will not waver when you walk through the storms of life that would tempt you to question the nature and integrity of God's goodness. In fact, your faith will be strengthened as His nature, integrity, and goodness are intrinsically expressed through you in the face of trials. It is the reason James says that we can "count it all joy when you face trials of many kinds"—you are being made perfect, just like your Father.

> GOD DID NOT MAKE OUR NEW HEARTS DECEITFUL AND DESPERATELY SICK. HE MADE US ONE WITH HIM, LIKE HIM, BEARING HIS IMAGE!

It is in the strength of this covenant that we are able to righteously and victoriously walk out the Christian life. When we begin to grasp this truth, we will find that our striving ceases and our intimacy with God grows tremendously. We no longer struggle to do Christian activities and ministry. We simply rest in our identity as sons and daughters of God, realizing that God is for us, that He created us in Christ for good works, which He prepared beforehand that we should walk in them. We will bear fruit effortlessly in this New Covenant as we allow ourselves to belong to God by simply abiding in the Vine that is Jesus Christ (John 15:5).

CHAPTER 5

RELATING TO GOD AS OUR FATHER

"Jesus said to her, "Do not cling to me, for I have not yet ascended to the Father; but go to my brothers and say to them, 'I am ascending to my Father and your Father, to my God and your God.'"

John 20:17

As we renew our minds in the truth and identity of being sons and daughters of God, receiving things from Him becomes inferior to actually knowing and being with Him. To have us in His family and to be in fellowship with us is His desire, and when we see this clearly, we will be provoked and compelled by love to seek and know Him more.

When the disciples wanted to learn how to pray, Jesus unveiled the intimacy of the New Covenant to them through modeling how to relate to God in a way that was inconceivable before that time. The new revelation that Jesus brought by presenting the God of Abraham, Isaac and Jacob as "Our Father" is one of the most significant in all the Scriptures.

Jesus instructs His disciples, "Pray then like this: 'Our Father in heaven...'" (Matt. 6:9). Jesus reveals God as the Father of all those who would believe in and receive Him, and not merely as His own Father or the Father of Israel. When Jesus was raised from the dead we see one of the most remarkable verses in the Bible: "Jesus said to her, 'Do not cling to me, for I have not yet ascended to the Father; but go to my brothers and say to them, 'I am ascending to my Father and your Father, to my God and your God.'" (John 20:17)

Can you hear the triumph in His voice? Can you imagine the twinkle in His eye? He comes roaring back to life, and one of the first things He says to Mary is to go tell the brothers that "My Father is now *your* father and that my God is now *your* God! Though you don't understand it yet, We have made a way for you to actually be born into Our family so that you can call God your very own Father." I honestly believe this is one of the most powerful revelations of the gospel. If we understand this deep relational connection that we have with God as Father, it will change the way we live, pray, and share the Good News with the world.

RELATIONSHIP LEADS TO REST

When God first started revealing this truth to my heart, my prayer life was turned upside-down, and I didn't understand why. I found myself not knowing what things to pray for since my heart was being established in the rest of truly belonging in God's family. I no longer felt like an outsider beseeching a distant God, hoping that my words and the posture of my heart were just right and that He would be stirred to act on my behalf. Instead of asking God to change circumstances or do things for me, I found myself at rest just being with Him. It was as if being with Him was all my soul really wanted, and the things I used to pray for became less important. At first I thought something was wrong because I no longer felt the familiar urge to petition God for things. Before then I had only known prayer to be that of coming to God with a list of things that I wanted or hoped would change. I foolishly believed that my requests would be answered based on the sincerity and length of my prayers. I would have never admitted it out loud, but this was the attitude of my heart.

I was deceived, believing that God was withholding from me unless I positioned myself in the exact way He wanted. Once I started to believe that the God of the universe was my Father, I found it difficult to even ask Him for the very things for which I used to beg. It seemed like the moment I turned my heart toward Him and rested in my identity as His son, I already had what I was looking for all along. It is as Paul writes in Romans 8:32, "If He gave us Christ, how will He not, along with Him, freely give us all things?"

When we truly grasp how the gospel takes us and lovingly places us into the family of God, through the broken body of Jesus Christ, we will realize that we are established in a place of favor and blessing with God. Our posture in prayer is not as important as what He has done on our behalf. I am not diminishing the joy of posturing ourselves before God in humility, brokenness, and utter dependence, but we do this because He first loved us. Paul explains this relationship to the church in Ephesus:

> *"For this reason I bow my knees before the Father, from whom every family in heaven and on earth is named, that according to the riches of His glory he may grant you to be strengthened with power through His Spirit in your inner being, so that Christ may dwell in your hearts through faith—that you, being rooted and grounded in love, may have strength to comprehend with all the saints what is the breadth and length and height and depth, and to know the love of Christ that surpasses knowledge, that you may be filled with all the fullness of God." (Eph. 3:14-19)*

It is because God is now our Father and we are co-heirs with Christ that we come to Him with bended knee, with honor, worship, and love in our hearts. When we come to Him, it is not so that we can get things from Him—it is simply to enjoy fellowship with Him. In the place of fellowship, we will develop a confident faith that everything in our Father's house now belongs to us. If the foundation of your prayer life (to receive "things" from God) is "how you come" or "how often you come" or "how long you stay," then you will always feel like you did not come in the right way, come often enough, or stay long enough. You will feel as if you are on a hamster wheel of spiritual activity, trying to find the right "formula" to get God to do what you think should be done. All the while, He just wants us to come to Him and find rest for our souls. The "things" we desire from Him will be sorted out by simply abiding in His presence.

It is in the intimate moments of fellowship with the Godhead, simply delighting in the gospel and the fact that we have been thoroughly cleansed by the blood of Jesus and made one with the Holy Spirit, that we will discover that anything is possible. We know that whatever we ask will be given to us because we are in the most privileged place in all the universe, the heart of our Father. I think this is perhaps the greatest privilege of being a Christian. We find our home in God's heart, and the reality of His heart overwhelms and overcomes anything we could possibly face in this life. Our lustful and carnal desires for the things of this world drastically fade away because of the joy that overtakes us being in such close proximity and oneness with God.

WHEN WE COME TO HIM, IT IS NOT SO THAT WE CAN GET THINGS FROM HIM—IT IS SIMPLY TO ENJOY FELLOWSHIP WITH HIM.

There is a belief I have found in the Church that blinds us to the generosity and kindness of our Father. It's the belief that what we do and how well we serve God will cause Him to be more or less generous with His affections and blessing. We come to this belief "honestly" because it is the "way that seems right to man" (Prov. 14:12).

We are trained from the time we are young that we get what we deserve or that we receive only to the measure that we work. We receive praises for doing things rightly and are disciplined for performing poorly. I know some could interpret this to an extreme and presume that what we do does not matter and that God does not require obedience to be pleased, but that is not what I am saying. I am suggesting that our serving God does nothing to open His heart toward us any more than it already is open.

THE PRODIGAL SON

The parable of the prodigal son in Luke 15 illustrates the irrevocable grace and generosity of the Father quite well. We know that the prodigal son asks for his inheritance prematurely so that he can go and spend it in reckless living. When he has exhausted all the money and finds himself in the midst of a severe famine, feeding pigs, he comes to his senses and realizes he could become a servant in his father's house and experience a better quality of life than his current state. As he heads toward home and comes within eyeshot of the family estate, his father immediately takes off running toward his wayward son. Upon meeting, the son begins to confess his failures and to humble himself before his father. The son declares that he is willing to become a servant in his father's house, but the father seems to ignore it all as he focuses on embracing his wayward son and celebrate his homecoming. The father shouts to his servants to bring the family ring, the robe, and fresh sandals. The father commences to lavish and celebrate this son of his by killing the fattened calf and throwing a massive party.

I think many of us can relate to God having lavished us in a similar manner when we "came home" and surrendered our lives to Jesus for the first time. The sense of peace, forgiveness, and love we felt from our Heavenly Father was overwhelming. Having all of our sins forgiven and being sealed with the Holy Spirit is an experience that is hard to describe. This is the joy of salvation, knowing that our Father in heaven celebrates us and welcomes us into his family, not as servants but as His very children! This is a beautiful picture and an experience we should regularly recall and give thanks for, no matter how long we have been in God's family.

THE OLDER SON

If we keep reading, we find another son in the story, who illustrates what I am talking about very clearly. The older brother of the prodigal son hears the sound of a party as he is returning to the house from working in the fields. He inquires of one of the servants as to what this sound could mean, and when he finds out that his father is celebrating the prodigal, wayward son by killing the fattened calf, he becomes incensed. We don't see his underlying belief system until the father invites the elder son to join the party. Immediately we can see a mindset unfold in this older brother that unfortunately has permeated much of the body of Christ. Let's look at the conversation they have in Luke 15:28-32:

> *"But he was angry and refused to go in. His father came out and entreated him, but he answered his father, 'Look, these many years* I have served you, *and* I never disobeyed your command, yet you never gave *me a young goat, that I might celebrate with my friends. But when this son of yours came, who has devoured your property with prostitutes, you killed the fattened calf for him!' And he said to him, 'Son, you are always with me, and all that is mine is yours. It was fitting to celebrate and be glad, for this your brother was dead, and is alive; he was lost, and is found.'"* (emphasis added)

Do you see it? The older son believed something about his father that inhibited him from receiving all that the father had for him. In just a few sentences, the son reveals two things about the posture of his heart toward his father. He says,

1. "I have served you."
2. "I have never disobeyed your command."
3. "Yet you never gave."

This son believed that his faithful service and obedience should have provoked his father to give him something. Through the father's response, we learn that the father was never withholding from the son, but that the son's belief about their relationship actually caused him to never ask anything from his father, and thus he never received. I believe the father's response is a remarkable portrayal of what our Heavenly Father is speaking to His children in this hour. We have not because we ask not. Hear it again and allow it to sink deep into your heart: "You are always with me, and all that is mine is yours."

Wow! The father in the parable declares that everything was at the older son's fingertips had he simply asked, knowing that his father loved him and desired to lavish him too! The prodigal son simply came home and received a full blessing from his father. He once again positioned himself as a son. In the father's mind, his generosity toward either son was not contingent upon their work in the fields or obedience to his commands; his lavish benevolence was always available because they were sons *with* him. The whole estate, everything in the father's possession, belonged to the older son without him even knowing it! What a tragedy! Think of all the dinner parties and joyous celebrations the older son could have enjoyed if he had only understood the access he had to the kindness and joy of his father through the relational connection he had to him as his son. I sometimes wonder if the older son was actually too busy working in the fields, thinking he was earning something from his father, all the while the father wanted to just *be* with his son.

We have churches and ministries filled with the sons and daughters of God, who serve faithfully and strive diligently to walk in obedience to our Father in heaven, believing their devotion should merit blessings and favor from God. There is obviously nothing wrong with serving God faithfully; in fact, service, passion, and obedience to God is an overflow of love and should be celebrated! However, our receiving from God is not tied to any actions on our part. Our receiving from God hinges solely on Jesus Christ and the work He has accomplished on our behalf in bringing us completely into the family of God. Because of His perfect work on the cross, we now belong to our Father in heaven, having been reconciled by the cross and saved by His resurrected life (Romans 5:10). This means that everything that the Father has belongs to us as His children.

> "YOU ARE ALWAYS WITH ME, AND ALL THAT IS MINE IS YOURS."

That we would be given so much for doing so little seems unfathomable and wildly unfair. This is the reason it depends exclusively on God's grace, so that none of us may boast (Eph. 2:9)! It is with great humility that we believe we belong in the family of God and, as such, have all access to His generosity.

If the older son served faithfully for his entire life yet didn't gain any more favor or access to his father's blessings as a result, it is safe to say that even if he had faltered in his service or obedience, he would not have been penalized relationally by his father. This could be an alarming revelation to parents, pastors, and others in positions of authority who may worry that people could use this as an excuse to sin. But I believe that quite the opposite will happen when we comprehend and embrace our position as sons and daughters of God. When we are confident in the truth that we belong to the God in heaven who calls us His own, we will gladly serve Him and walk in obedience. Because we love Him and identify as His children, it will be our delight to honor Him in righteousness. It is from this identity that we will also see our Father's willingness to freely give us all things.

THE DESIRE FOR DIESEL

There was a time in my life that I really wanted to drive a large diesel truck. I had always owned old, beat-up cars, and for some reason I loved the idea of driving a large pickup truck. I live in Texas after all! I had shared this with a few people, but one divine weekend I was spending some time with my older brother and his family in Houston, Texas, and something unexpected happened. When I woke up, my brother asked if he could speak with me for a moment, and it seemed rather serious. He called me into his bedroom and told me that, as he was praying, the LORD had prompted him to give to me a brand-new truck that he intended to purchase later that week. His heart was to let me drive it for a year before he used it, simply to bless me. As you can imagine, my jaw hit the floor.

I realized two things that day. My Father in heaven knows and cares about all of the little, seemingly insignificant desires of my heart, and secondly, my brother hears the voice of God! What a glorious gift and extravagant act of kindness!

Later that weekend we drove to the dealership to pick up the truck. It was more beautiful than I had imagined. A pristine Ford F-250 Diesel 4x4 truck with black leather interior and a bright beautiful blue paint job was more than I could handle! I hadn't been praying or fasting for God to give me a truck, and I didn't earn that truck through my faithful service to God. My Father in heaven simply wanted to bless me and used my older brother to do it! It was evidence of what Paul says in Romans 8:32, "He who did not spare His own Son, but gave Him up for us all—how will He not also, along with Him, graciously give us all things?"

CHAPTER 6

BORN AGAIN WITH A DIVINE NATURE

"I'm not afraid of the devil. The devil can handle me - he's got judo I never heard of. But he can't handle the One to whom I'm joined; he can't handle the One to whom I'm united; he can't handle the One whose nature dwells in my nature."

A. W. Tozer

Much of Christianity found in Western culture has tragically evolved into a vague moral code that entails going to church and trying to do the "right" thing. But the passion displayed through the gospel, redeeming mankind out of sin and into the family of God, is so intense and marvelous that the Christian life must reflect the beauty and joy of this sacrifice at some level. The Godhead went to great lengths to purchase us out of death and into eternal life. For too long the gospel has been reduced to praying a prayer in a moment of sincerity to receive a heavenly passport that will be given to us when we die. We have overemphasized eternal destiny and minimized the overall process of life transformation that takes place through the gospel.

This reduction of the gospel has been ingrained into the hearts and minds of believers who, as a result, no longer see how the gospel applies to their everyday life. We should never grow up so much that we outgrow the beauty of the gospel; it is integral to our Christian walk. It is the Good News that continually reminds us of our hope, freedom, and salvation. To no longer apply its power throughout our Christian life is to scorn the gift of righteousness and ignore the saving power of God in our body, soul, and spirit.

TEMPLES OF GOD

One of the most marvelous realities in the New Covenant is that our bodies have become God's literal dwelling place on the earth. We see this truth in the following passages:

> *"Don't you know that your body is a temple of the Holy Spirit within you, whom you have from God?" (1 Cor. 6:19)*
>
> *"But you are a chosen race, a royal priesthood, a holy nation, a people for His own possession, that you may proclaim the excellencies of Him who called you out darkness into His marvelous light." (1 Pet. 2:9)*

The presence of God with the people of Israel is what consecrated or set them apart from all the other nations in the earth. It is the same today. The presence of the Holy Spirit in the hearts of believers distinguishes us from every other group of people on planet earth. We see this in Moses's words: "For how shall it be known that I have found favor in your sight, I and your people? Is it not in your going with us, so that we are distinct [set apart], I and your people, from every other people on the face of the earth?" (Ex. 33:16).

The presence of God now dwelling in the hearts of men is one of the most profound mysteries revealed in the New Covenant. I was once doing a study on the book of 1 & 2 Samuel alongside a study of the book of Hebrews. One morning I read 2 Samuel 6, which tells the story of David and his men attempting to bring back the Ark of the Covenant to the city of Jerusalem. The Ark of the Covenant was an ornate wooden box that literally contained the presence of God Himself. It was placed in the temple, where sacrifices and other forms of worship were offered to God. When the Ark was taken by enemies from the City of God, it was the desire of King David to bring it back to the capital city of Jerusalem.

In 2 Samuel 6, we learn that God had determined a very specific way for the Ark to be moved around. Instead of consulting the Scriptures, David simply assembled some men and had the ark placed on a wooden cart that was carried by oxen. David appointed a handful of men to make sure the Ark was safely carried back to Jerusalem. Well, as it happened, one of the oxen stumbled while carrying the Ark, and a man named Uzzah, a friend of David's, put out his hand to stabilize the Ark so it wouldn't fall to the ground. As he did, the presence of God consumed Uzzah, and he died on the spot. David was distraught, and the mission failed. They took the Ark aside, to the house of a man named Obed-Edom, where it remained for some time.

As I continued my studies, later that same day I was reading in the book of Hebrews about the New Covenant and about how the blood of Jesus has thoroughly cleansed the hearts of men so that they can become carriers of the presence of God. As I was reading about these amazing truths, I imagined myself in the scene described in 2 Samuel 6. I was standing before King David just moments after Uzzah had died. I could tell that David was terribly distraught and discouraged by what had happened.

I approached King David and told him that I was from the future. I pointed to the Ark of the Covenant, and I said, "Do you see the Ark? That lives inside of me right now." David said, "That's impossible." He clearly could not understand how his friend merely touched the Ark and died in a moment, and yet I could claim that this Holy, All-Consuming Fire named Yahweh could dwell inside of a mere mortal. I continued to explain to David that many years later God would actually send His own Son as a sacrificial Lamb to be killed as a sin offering for all of mankind. He began to understand as soon as I started talking about sin-offerings.

I told King David, "God's own Son shed His blood to cleanse the hearts of mankind. He has made us perfectly clean and completely holy, so that He could be as close to us as He has always wanted to be. That nearness was manifested on the Day of Pentecost when He sent the Holy Spirit, God Himself, in the hearts of 120 men and women, with a mighty wind and a flame of fire."

It was after this vision that I began to understand the power of the blood of Jesus to cleanse a human heart, preparing it to become a living tabernacle for God Himself. This reality has changed my life more than any other reality and has laid the foundation for me to understand the new divine nature we have when we are born of God and He dwells within us.

A NEW AND DIVINE NATURE

The literal indwelling of the Holy Spirit is the grounds upon which we become partakers of the divine nature. I believe that understanding the divine nature is key to living out and experiencing our salvation. As the old revivalist John G. Lake once said, "The secret to the Christian life is not in doing, but in being."[1] If we understand that through the gospel, God has imparted to us His very nature (His righteousness and likeness) by the Holy Spirit, then all we have to do is abide in Him and imitate what we see (Eph. 5:1-2).

What a beautiful picture this is! When we are born again we are given a new nature, a Divine nature, that comes from God. What if, instead of trying to control people into behaving properly and walk-

[1] John G. Lake, *John G. Lake: The Complete Collection of His Life Teachings*, comp. Roberts Liardon (New Kensington, PA: Whitaker House, 2005).

ing within the lines of a legalistic religiosity, we helped them to see their true identity in Christ and gave them grace and freedom to walk it out? If someone has put his faith in Jesus Christ and has sincerely made Him his Lord and Savior, then the Bible quite expressly says that he has become a brand-new creature (2 Cor. 5:17), a partaker of the Divine nature (2 Pet. 1:4), filled with the life and substance of God Himself (1 Cor. 6:19), and equipped by the Holy Spirit with everything he needs for life and godliness (2 Peter 1:3). He has full access to the Holy of Holies through the torn veil of the Body of Jesus Christ, and every spiritual blessing has been bestowed upon him in Christ. God does not partially save; that person has been thoroughly cleansed and filled by God to the uttermost.

Not comprehending this New Covenant reality has led many to believe a veiled, inaccurate gospel message that gives people very little permission or encouragement to believe it is possible to live free from sin, sickness, death, and every other consequence of the fall of man. Now is the time that God is raising up men and women who preach and live a gospel that promises and demonstrates a mighty salvation! The days of being dominated by the devil are over. Salvation has come. We are destined to be a people of victory, strength, hope, and life! I am not preaching a blessed life apart from trials, tribulations, or storms. On the contrary, we enter the Kingdom of God with much difficulty (Acts 14:22). But, because the gospel connects us permanently to the heart of God by the Holy Spirit, it can bring us powerfully through every trial and storm that we may face.

GOOD VIBES

One day I was meditating on this reality, thinking about how God has taken up residence in my physical body by the Holy Spirit. I began to think about how God loves everyone even though I am not always in tune with that reality. So I walked into a Starbucks thinking about the God of Love dwelling in my physical body, and, as I walked in with a smile on my face, the young girl behind the counter said, "Wow, you have some good vibes coming off of you." Her face lit up with a smile as she said it, curious as to who I was and why she felt so happy all of a sudden.

Not really knowing what to say or do (that hasn't happened too often), I just told her, "That's Jesus, He lives in me and He loves you. That's what you are feeling." To my surprise, she said, "I should've known that!" We both laughed. Because God lives in us by the Holy Spirit, His presence can be felt and experienced tangibly by others.

GOD CAN BRING US POWERFULLY THROUGH EVERY TRIAL AND STORM.

CHAPTER 7
ETERNAL LIFE

"For God so loved the world that He gave His only begotten son that whosoever believes in Him shall not perish but have eternal life."

John 3:16

For as long as I can remember, I have equated the phrase "eternal life" with a promise of going to heaven when I die. The longer I've been a Christian, the more of God's Word I have studied, and the more intently I meditate on the holistic saving power of the gospel, I am convinced that this understanding of eternal life does not do it justice. Eternal life speaks of something much greater than being whisked to heaven when we die. If eternal life is simply going to heaven when we die, then we should call it life after death rather than eternal life. You might be wondering, *What is the difference? Why split hairs?*

I do believe that going to heaven when we die is mind-blowing and one of the most glorious promises in the gospel. No matter what happens, we can rest assured that our final destination is the presence of God in His glorious Kingdom. The problem I have with the traditional understanding of the phrase "eternal life" is that I don't believe it captures the fullness of what God intends to impart to us through

His Son. If His end-goal is to get us to heaven, then He could have just raptured us to be with Him the very moment we put our faith in Him.

ABUNDANT LIFE

Going to heaven is included in the promise of eternal life, but it is not the sum total of the eternal life that I believe God has for us. Looking at John 10:10, we can begin to understand the glorious enormity of eternal life: "The thief comes only to steal and kill and destroy. I came that they may have life and have it abundantly."

Here we get closer to what God desires to impart to us through His Son: abundant life, eternal abundant life. I believe that the promise of the gospel, to those who receive the Son, is a life on this earth of such quality, strength, and vibrancy that whatever evil comes against us will be overcome by the powerful life God has given us. What do I mean? I mean that the promise of eternal life doesn't start once we die but in the moment we acknowledge Jesus as our Lord and Savior, the same moment we receive the Holy Spirit who is the conduit for eternal life. The Holy Spirit beckons us to come underneath the rivers of living water that flow from His presence, so that our once-darkened hearts can be put to death and resurrected to new life, abundant life, eternal life. This exchange incites a vibrant, lively river flowing from of our inmost being, as John writes: "Whoever believes in me, as Scripture has said, 'Out of his heart will flow rivers of living water'" (John 7:38).

ABUNDANCE FOR OTHERS

The abundant eternal life is not solely for us but also for the world around us. It consists of a heavenly substance, the divine life of God, and allows us to be a blessing to the world around us. God did not just bless us and give us His Spirit without measure so we could have a nice church meeting or occasionally experience goose bumps. He fills us with Himself so that rivers of abundant life flow from us and into the world around us. When we see eternal life as a daily present reality and not something we have after this life on earth, we will realize we have so much more to give than we thought.

HE FILLS US WITH HIMSELF, MAKING RIVERS OF ABUNDANT LIFE FLOW FROM US AND INTO THE WORLD AROUND US.

Practically speaking, sharing the abundant life with others can be rather easy. Proverbs 18 says that the power of life and death is in the tongue, which means we have the power to release this life over others by what we speak. Combine that with 1 John 3:18, which says, "Little children, let us not love in word or talk but in deed and in truth," and we see a Christian who is not only speaking life and blessing over people but also demonstrating that same life!

LIFE IN OUR TONGUE

One day, while at my wife's parents' house, I went for a run. During the run I was communing with the Lord, and I became very encouraged in my spirit through a time of worship and prayer as I ran through the park. When I got back to the house, there was a young man dressed in all black in the neighbor's yard doing some work on the lawn. I immediately felt the compassion of the Lord for him, as it was apparent to me that he was carrying a very heavy load. His countenance and posture reflected a man who had carried the weight of his mistakes and shortcomings for a long time. I walked right up to him and asked him if he would allow me to share some things with him. He permitted me to do so, and I began to speak something like this over his life:

"Your life has a purpose and destiny. You're not a failure. God loves you so much, and He's not angry with your inability to do the right things; He just wants you to know that He loves you, and He is for you, and He most certainly will redeem all the pain and difficulty you have had. Your life is not a mistake, and I pray that God will reveal His great purpose for your life and draw you close to Himself."

The young man looked a little startled at the direct and pointed way in which I encouraged him, but I was assured he heard what I said and was, at least in some way, very encouraged. I had never met this young man before and had no expectation that I would see him again, as my wife's parents live in a different town than the one in which I live.

Six months passed and I was on my way to work one day, walking down the city block to my office. I don't remember why, but I was feeling very discouraged that day. Since I had just heard a message on "binding and loosing," I decided that I would try to put this principle into practice in hopes that I could somehow encounter God's heart and His optimism in that moment. I prayed this simple prayer, "Father, I bind a spirit of discouragement, and I loose a spirit of encouragement over my life."

As God is my witness, after one minute of praying this prayer, I received a call from my mother-in-law. Now, some people might not think that is encouraging, but I love my mother-in-law, and I thought this indeed might be an answer to my prayer. She got right to the point and asked me, "Did you pray for my neighbor's son?" Confused as to what she was asking me, I asked her to clarify what she was trying to say. She told me, "Well, my neighbor called me and told me that one of my sons prayed for her son and that ever since that prayer, he has turned his life around. She said they had been praying for him to be saved for years, and ever since you spoke to him, he has gotten right with God, lost weight, stopped smoking, and started going to hair school to make something of his life. His mom just called to thank me for your prayers and to let me know what happened."

Needless to say, I was wildly encouraged, both by this radical testimony of transformation in a young man's life as well as the power and immediate change that took place when I loosed a spirit of encouragement over my own life! Proverbs says that the power of life and death is in our tongues, and I think this testimony illustrates the power that we have to release life over another human being. Undoubtedly my words were empowered by the many prayers that had been prayed by his family, but my words were like a match that lit the gasoline of prayers that had been saturating him for years! Bless the Lord!

The only member of the Godhead on planet earth to reveal the Father and the Son to us is the Holy Spirit. He is the One who makes His home in our hearts (1 Cor. 6:16, Rom. 5:5), comforts us (John 14:16), and leads and guides us into all Truth (John 16:13). Eternal life is the life of God that is so strong that, if death comes knocking on our door to overtake our physical body, the eternal life given to us plows through its grip and ushers us into the loving arms of our Savior. It is like a freight train that cannot be stopped or contained. Like a roaring river, it will powerfully flow from our lives if we will just surrender ourselves to be overcome by it.

Many people desire to have this adventurous life of faith but are unwilling to yield to it. They choose instead to maintain an "orderly" life because in doing so they can preserve a sense of control. I have found that to truly experience this abundant, eternal life, we must be willing to meet God on His terms. We must yield to the Holy Spirit and be willing to walk in His ways. We must learn to hear and obey His voice, not only to be made righteous but to intimately know Him, which is the eternally abundant life.

CHAPTER 8

OVERVIEW OF JUSTIFICATION, SANCTIFICATION, AND GLORIFICATION

"Now I would remind you, brothers, of the gospel I preached to you, which you received, in which you stand, and by which you are being saved, if you hold fast to the word I preached to you—unless you believed in vain."

1 Corinthians 15:1-3

Understanding why we are saved, what we are saved from and what we are saved into is a wonderful foundation for understanding *how* we are saved. Being familiar with the how of salvation is crucial to standing in and experiencing the daily power of salvation. There are two sides to the same coin that we must look at to see the full picture. The first side of the coin is understanding how God effectually saves us. We know that His motive in saving us is love (why) and the promised land that He saves us into (what) is the New Covenant with all of its blessings. Having looked at many of the promises and blessings inherent with the New Covenant, it begs the question for most of us, "How do I actually experience so great a salvation?" Fortunately, the Bible is very clear on this, and I will devote the next portion of this book to exploring this in depth.

TRIUNE GRACE FOR THE TRIPLE CURSE

God's method of salvation is supplied to us by what I would like to call a triune grace. This triune grace is the saving power of God manifested to each believer to deliver from sin, sickness, death, and all other collateral damage from the Fall of Man. John G. Lake in describing the works of the devil said this:

> *"Sin, sickness and death are doomed, doomed to death by the decree of Christ Jesus. Sin, sickness and death are the devil's triumvirate--the triple curse. Heaven is the absence of this triple curse; heaven is sinlessness, sicklessness and deathlessness. This is the ultimate of Christ's redemption."* [2]

Now hear how the Bible speaks of Christ's victory over the devil:

> *"The last enemy to be destroyed is death." (1 Cor. 15:26)*
>
> *"The reason the Son of God appeared was to destroy the works of the devil." (1 John 3:8)*

God's triune grace brings the reality of heaven to our lives and is distributed in many aspects of our salvation. Initially and instantly, the first aspect of this triune grace is manifest in what we call justification, the saving of our spirits from the penalty of death. The second part of this triune grace is distributed by God through sanctification, which is God's way of imparting the righteousness of Christ to our very souls. The final aspect of this triune grace is called glorification and will not be fully manifest until Christ returns and the "mortal puts on the immortal" (1 Cor. 15:54).

So if justification is our rebirth back into the image and likeness of God, then our sanctification is our growing up and learning how

[2] John G. Lake, *John G. Lake: The Complete Collection of His Life Teachings*, comp. Roberts Liardon (New Kensington, PA: Whitaker House, 2005).

to think, act, and feel as a child of God. And, finally, that makes our glorification, the fullness of which we will experience when Christ returns, the completion and maturation of what we were always meant to be. We see, through this explanation, that God's idea of salvation is much more deep and complete than simply going to heaven when we die.

> IF JUSTIFICATION IS OUR REBIRTH INTO THE IMAGE AND LIKENESS OF GOD, THEN OUR SANCTIFICATION IS OUR GROWING UP INTO THINKING, ACTING, AND FEELING AS A CHILD OF GOD.

SAVED BY GRACE - THROUGH FAITH

The other side of the coin in the "how" of salvation is how we access or experience this triune saving grace. It is evident that just because God has purposed to save us, it does not mean that all, in fact, are saved. So how is it that people can enter into and experience the grace that God so graciously offers us through His Son? We should be clear here that the triune grace is the actual power of God which brings about the transformation in our lives and allows us to truly experience the gift of righteousness in our entire being. In order to access this power, we must look to the Word of God to see how this triune grace is imparted to each one of us. Paul writes, "For *by grace* you have been saved *through faith*" (Eph. 2:8, emphasis added). We see here that this grace is only accessed through faith. Faith is the key to accessing this triune power of God's grace that brings about a real salvation. If faith is the key to accessing God's triune grace, then let us establish what faith is, according to His word: "So faith comes by hearing, and hearing through the word of Christ" (Rom. 10:17) and "...looking to Jesus, the founder and perfecter of our faith..." (Heb. 12:2).

When some people think of "having faith," they often associate it with some spiritual work or action they must do. We have associated people of "great faith" with the spiritual disciplines or radical risks that have accompanied their lives instead of looking at and understanding the true Source of their faith. According to the two verses above, we see that faith comes to a person through "hearing the word of Christ" and by "looking at Jesus." It is through the hearing of the Word that we are given the invitation to simply believe. Faith can be birthed through the spiritual discipline of reading the Word every day, but that spiritual discipline, or others like it, do not necessarily produce faith. It is possible to hear the word of Christ and harden our hearts in unbelief, rendering us immobile and unable to enter the promise of salvation. The author of Hebrews says it this way: "Today, if you hear His voice, do not harden your hearts as in the rebellion...So we see that they were unable to enter because of unbelief...For good news came to us just as to them, but the message they heard did not benefit them, because they were not united by faith with those who listened" (Heb. 3:15, 19; Heb. 4:2).

This shows us that faith does, in fact, come by hearing and that the condition of our hearts plays a vital role in either stepping into the grace offered by God through the Word or by rejecting the same through unbelief. However, it is not just the condition of our hearts and the hearing of the Word that impacts our ability to have faith. As we read in Hebrews 12, we see that in "looking to Jesus," we find Him as the "founder" and the "perfecter" of our faith. So it is not only in hearing the word of Christ that the door of faith is opened to us, but it is in beholding the man Jesus Christ. We find that as we gaze upon Him and His beauty, faith is not only birthed in our hearts but it will also be perfected. So for the sake of clarity and brevity, we can conclude that faith comes by both hearing the word of Christ and by looking to Jesus, through prayer, worship, and adoration.

JOHN WESLEY'S CONVERSION

A brief scene from John Wesley's conversion story clearly illustrates the evidence or fruit of a true saving faith. One of the Moravians by the name of Peter Boehler explained to Wesley that there were two distinct and inseparable fruits of having faith in Christ:

"So that when Peter Boehler, whom God prepared for me as soon as I came to London, affirmed of true faith in Christ, (which is but one,) that it had those two fruits inseparably attending it, 'Dominion over sin, and constant Peace from a sense of forgiveness,' I was quite amazed, and looked upon it as a new gospel."

Like Wesley, the gospel that many of us heard only promised the forgiveness of past sins and eternity in heaven but offered no real dominion over sin or constant peace from having been thoroughly forgiven and cleansed of all unrighteousness (1 John 1:9). As I stated earlier, forgiveness of past sins and eternity in heaven are profound and most definite blessings of the gospel. However, what I feel many have not understood is that the life and work of Christ in saving mankind is itself triune in nature. God has saved us (past tense) through Christ's work on the cross; He is saving us (present tense) through the life and ministry of Christ, made effective by the Holy Spirit; and, finally, God will save us (future tense) completely at the end of this age. If we only preach and teach one aspect of His work and life, then it will be impossible to have faith in the other parts because we have not yet heard them! There is a story in Acts 18-19 that illustrates this point very well.[1]

Edwin And Jennifer Woodruff Tait et al., "The Moravians and John Wesley," Christian History | Learn the History of Christianity & the Church, , accessed December 29, 2016, http://www.christianitytoday.com/history/issues/issue-1/moravians-and-john-wesley.html.

APOLLOS' INCOMPLETE GOSPEL

There was a man by the name of Apollos, whom the Bible describes as an "eloquent man, competent in the Scriptures, instructed in the way of the Lord, fervent in spirit and accurately teaching the things of Jesus" (see Acts 18:24-25). However, it was said of this man that he only knew the baptism of John. Apollos was preaching boldly in the synagogues, turning people to Jesus and making disciples, but because he was not preaching the entire gospel, a couple by the name of Priscilla and Aquila took him aside and "explained to him the way of God more accurately" (Acts 18:26).

> *"And it happened that while Apollos was at Corinth, Paul passed through the inland country and came to Ephesus. There he found some disciples. And he said to them, 'Did you receive the Holy Spirit when you believed?' And they said, 'No, we have not even heard that there is a Holy Spirit.' And he said, 'Into what then were you baptized?' They said, 'Into John's baptism.' And Paul said, 'John baptized with the baptism of repentance, telling the people to believe in the one who was to come after him, that is, Jesus.' On hearing this, they were baptized in the name of the Lord Jesus. And when Paul had laid his hands on them, the Holy Spirit came on them, and they began speaking in tongues and prophesying." (Acts 19:1-6)*

In the instance depicted here Apollos was fervent, eloquent and sincere, yet he was not preaching the fullness of the gospel. Because he himself was limited in his understanding of the work of Christ, being ignorant of the baptism of the Holy Spirit, the disciples he was making were just as clueless. The grace and power of the Holy Spirit was available to them at all times, but because no one had explained to them that specific work of Christ (the Baptism of the Holy Spirit), they were unable to experience that grace. Likewise, today, it is possible that many believers are not walking in the victorious, whole salvation of their spirit, souls, and bodies because they have not yet heard all that is available to them through the work of Jesus!

In the following chapters we will look closely at the entire work of Christ and the grace that it now gives us access to by faith.

CHAPTER 9

THE JUSTIFYING GRACE

"Justification and regeneration are simultaneous. The pardoned sinner becomes a child of God in justification."

William J. Seymour

Our concept and understanding of what it means to be "saved" has been so limited that it is no wonder that we have failed to truly enter into and possess all of the promises that belong to us in Christ. The justifying grace of God, purchased by the work of Jesus in His crucifixion, burial, and resurrection, is an all-consuming one that meets sinful man, an enemy of God, declares him righteous, and thrusts him into the New Covenant with God, making him a brand-new creature, born again of God and in the likeness of God. This is the first aspect of salvation and is what most call their "conversion experience." In the same way that a child is conceived in the womb of a woman through the seed of a man, so the Christian is born again and justified through the Seed of Heaven, the Holy Spirit: "Since you have been born again, not of perishable seed but of imperishable, through the living and abiding word of God." (1 Peter 1:23)

It is only by first understanding that we have been justified, completely born again, and made new, that we will experience and access the other facets of salvation. In the same way that that sin entered into Adam but did not fully produce death in Adam until some 900 years later, when his physical body died, so it is with the righteousness of God. It takes time for the righteousness of God in our spirits to spread to our soul and body. Here's how I would define justification:

The gift of righteousness freely given to man in the form of a declaration by God ("You are righteous") to the one who has put their faith in and identified with the death, burial and resurrection of Jesus Christ.

To say that we are only righteous in God's sight (as opposed to being made inwardly righteous) is to grossly underestimate the power of the cross, baptism, and resurrection of Jesus. To hold this view is to say boldly that the crucifixion, burial, and resurrection of Christ is not sufficient or complete in purging and saving mankind from sin. Our justification is God legally proclaiming that the one who has been crucified, buried, and resurrected with Christ is now in fact righteous.

OUR JUSTIFICATION IS GOD LEGALLY PROCLAIMING THAT THE ONE WHO HAS BEEN BEEN CRUCIFIED, BURIED, AND RESURRECTED WITH CHRIST IS NOW IN FACT RIGHTEOUS.

When we receive the gift of righteousness in our spirits (justification), then we begin to walk in the grace of sanctification. This grace of sanctification causes the Seed of Heaven, the Holy Spirit, to manifest the character and nature of Christ (righteousness) in our souls. This is a process not of human effort and striving but of simply believing in and trusting in the living Christ to form His thoughts, desires, and emotions in our very own hearts through intimacy with our Creator.

JUSTIFIED BY BELIEF AND CONFESSION

The work of the cross (the death, burial, and resurrection of Jesus) gives us access to the grace of justification, which results in a glorious exchange of our sinful nature for the very righteousness of Christ, implanted by the Holy Spirit in our inmost being. This is God's way of delivering us from the penalty of sin, which is death. "For the wages of sin is death…" (Rom. 6:23). To understand the magnitude of this aspect of our salvation, we have to look very closely at how God has determined to implement this salvation to our spirits and how we appropriate this aspect of our redemption. The Bible is explicit in its expression that "Everyone who calls on the name of the Lord will be saved" (Rom. 10:13). Again, it says, "If you confess with your mouth that Jesus is Lord and believe in your heart that God raised Him from the dead, you will be saved. For with the heart one believes and is justified, and with the mouth one confesses and is saved" (Rom. 10:9-10). And, finally, in John 1:12 it says, "But to all who did receive Him, who believed in His name, He gave the right to become children of God, who were born, not of blood nor of the will of the flesh nor of the will of man, but of God."

In these three texts, we see that in order for each of us to enter into the promise of salvation, it is a necessity that we believe in our heart that Jesus is Lord, with a corresponding confession of our mouths. When this type of belief and confession takes place in a man's life, we know that God's power is ignited, and He immediately takes the very righteousness of Christ, by the Holy Spirit, and imparts it to the once-dead spirit of the man, making him instantaneously and gloriously alive to God in his inmost being, his spirit. The language the Bible uses to describe justification or conversion is "being born of God," "born again," or "partaking of the Divine nature" (John 1:12, John 3:3, 2 Peter 1:4). It's easy, then, to understand our justification as a rebirth into the nature and likeness of God.

"Blessed be the God and Father of our Lord Jesus Christ! According to His great mercy, He has caused us to be born again to a living hope through the resurrection of Jesus Christ from the dead." (1 Pet.1:3)

"Since you have been born again, not of perishable seed but of imperishable, through the living and abiding word of God." (1 Pet. 1:23)

DEATH OF THE SPIRIT

As we study all that Christ accomplished through His death and resurrection, we find that He was fully addressing the problem of sin from every angle and in every way in which humanity was affected by the fall of man. The initial effect of the Fall was the death of the spirit of Adam and Eve:

"And the Lord God commanded the man, saying, 'You may surely eat of every tree of the garden, but of the tree of the knowledge of good and evil, you shall not eat, for in the day that you eat of it you shall surely die.'" (Gen. 2:16-17)

From this passage, we know that the death that the Lord spoke of was a spiritual one, since Adam and Eve did not physically fall over and die the moment they ate of the tree. Sin came into the world through Adam and Eve's disobedience in eating of the tree of the knowledge of good and evil, and thus this condition of sin began to produce death in every aspect of humanity. A spiritual death took place immediately in Adam and Eve, which rendered them unable to continue the spiritual union with God that they had once enjoyed. As a result of this death in their spirits, shame consumed them, and we can see, as the beginning chapters of Genesis continue to unfold, that their spiritual deaths began to spread to their souls (mind, will, and emotions). Ultimately, hundreds of years later, this spiritual death would produce a physical death.

So we see that even from the beginning it took time for sin to become fully mature, or "fully grown," as the book of James describes it, and for that sin to eventually produce death in man's entire being. And so it is with our salvation, this journey of a living faith that connects us to God's triune grace until the nature and likeness of Christ is completely restored throughout our entire being.

"Therefore, my beloved, as you have always obeyed, so now, not only as in my presence but much more in my absence, work out your own salvation with fear and trembling, for it is God who works in you, both to will and to work for His good pleasure" (Phil. 2:12-13).

God takes the Holy Spirit that has been deposited into our spirits and begins to knead and mold our lives in such a way that the yeast of His Spirit would eventually leaven the whole lump. It is in yielding and trusting in this God who works in us that we will work out our salvation from our inmost being, into all aspects of our lives.

WORK OF ADAM VERSUS WORK OF JESUS

In Romans 5, Paul begins to explain how the "work of Adam" that produced sin and death in all men is met and overwhelmed by the work of Jesus.

> *"Therefore, as one trespass led to condemnation for all men, so one act of righteousness leads to justification and life for all men. For as by the one man's disobedience the many were made sinners, so by the one man's obedience the many will be made righteous." (Rom. 5:18-19)*

Gaining an understanding of how each aspect of the life (and death) of Christ addresses and atones for the penalty and consequences of sin will produce in us a great faith to enter into and experience the powerful and complete promise of salvation that God has offered us through His Son. Here we see that the spiritual death that came to man through Adam's disobedience, the curse, if you will, was met by the death and the blood of Jesus: "Since, therefore, we have now been justified by His blood ... For if while we were enemies we were reconciled to God by the death of His Son" (Rom. 5:9-10). Paul is explicit here that the death, the crucifixion, and the blood of Jesus gives us access to this grace of justification that makes our spirits, our inmost beings, as righteous as Christ Himself.

Some have argued that the "righteousness of God" that is conferred upon us through justification is merely a change in our legal standing before God but does not necessitate or produce a real change in our actual nature. Yet Paul says our nature is now made righteous: "Therefore, as one trespass led to condemnation for all men, so one act of righteousness leads to justification and life for all men. For as by the one man's disobedience the many were made sinners, so by the one man's obedience the many will be made righteous." (Rom. 5:18-19).

If the disobedience of Adam resulted in "the many [being made] sinners," which was a change, or deviation or perversion, of the original God-like nature, so "the one man's obedience" will definitely and most permanently result in "the many [being made] righteous" in their nature. Again Paul reiterates the strength and overwhelming work of Jesus in addressing the problem of sin:

> *"But the free gift is not like the trespass. For if many died through one man's trespass, much more have the grace of God and the free gift by the grace of that one man Jesus Christ abounded for many. And the free gift is not like the result of that one man's sin. For the one judgment following one trespass brought condemnation,*

> *but the free gift following many trespasses brought justification. For if, because of one man's trespass, death reigned through that one man, much more will those who receive the abundance of grace and the free gift of righteousness reign in life through the one man Jesus Christ." (Rom. 5:15-17)*

It is through receiving the abundance of grace and the free gift of righteousness that we reign in life, free from the dominion and power of sin, through the life of Jesus Christ imparted to us by the Holy Spirit.

So the question begs, if Christ has made us righteous through His death and blood, then why do people continue to sin? I believe it is because the entire gospel of God has not been communicated to them. In our haste to get people "converted" and redeemed from an eternal separation with God, we have not continued in our proclamation of the gospel message and have become lazy in our application and demonstration of this Good News to the believer! As the writer of Hebrews said, "Therefore we must pay much closer attention to what we have heard, lest we drift away from it" (Heb. 2:1). And again Paul reiterates in his letter to the Romans:

> *"What shall we say then? Are we to continue in sin that grace may abound? By no means! How can we who died to sin still live in it? Do you not know that all of us who have been baptized in Christ Jesus were baptized into his death? We were buried therefore with him by baptism into death, in order that, just as Christ was raised from the dead by the glory of the Father, we too might walk in newness of life." (Rom. 6:1-4)*

BAPTISM: CONSIDER YOURSELF DEAD TO SIN

If the blood justifies us and transforms our once-dead spirits into the very righteousness of God, then the actual burial of Jesus is what allows us to be "dead" to the sinful nature we once identified with.

Paul goes to great lengths to explain how the work of Christ in its many facets meets the need of humanity. The blood on the Mercy Seat (Heb. 9:5) brings us close and reconciles us to God, while His death and burial is what allows us to bury and consider ourselves completely dead to our old sinful nature. In this text we see that water baptism is so much more than a public proclamation of our faith, but it is a prophetic act in which we allow God, by the Holy Spirit, to destroy our old man through our identification with the death, burial and resurrection of Jesus. As Paul writes, "For if we have been united with Him in a death like His, we shall certainly be united with Him in a resurrection like His" (Rom. 6:5).

When we put our faith in Jesus Christ as our Lord and Savior, we have the privilege of identifying with His death through water baptism. This water baptism is so much more than a public proclamation of belief in Jesus; it is the burial of our old sinful nature through the finished work of Christ on the cross. Thus, as we enter the waters of baptism, Paul is urging us to have faith in the burial of Jesus, that our old sinful nature is buried with Christ, so that as we come up out of the waters, we, too, may identify with His resurrection (becoming a new creation), giving us access and grace to a new way of life apart from sin:

> *"We know that our old self was crucified with Him in order that the body of sin might be brought to nothing, so that we would no longer be enslaved to sin. For one who has died has been set free from sin. Now if we have died with Christ, we believe that we will also live with Him." (Rom 6:6-7)*

So if our justification brings life and righteousness to our once-dead spirits and imparts to us the divine nature, let's look at our new nature and the exhortations and instructions in God's Word that will renew our minds and allow us to live as new creations in Christ.

CHAPTER 10
NEW NATURE

"Therefore, if anyone is in Christ, he is a new creation. The old has passed away; behold, the new has come."

2 Corinthians 5:17

Since much of the Church today has equated the forgiveness of sins with the culmination of the gospel message, it could be unsettling for some to discover that the *forgiveness* of sins existed under the Old Covenant long before the blood of Jesus was shed. God, through Moses, made a covenant with Israel, which provided the people a way to receive forgiveness for their sins. I will not go into great detail about how forgiveness was obtained since there are too many details to list here, but the general procedure had to do with the killing of an unblemished animal in the presence of the High Priest. Depending on what type of sin was committed, a different animal and perhaps a slightly different procedure for each would be required. Regardless of the details, blood was shed, and then forgiveness for the sin would be offered to the offender.. In this way, the people of Israel maintained a clear conscience before God; that is, until they would break God's law again and be required to bring another sacrifice. This, of course, foreshadows the coming of Christ as our sacrificial Lamb.

There are other accounts in the Bible where the forgiveness of sins was offered prior to Jesus' blood being shed. One example was the coming of John the Baptist in the spirit of Elijah. John the Baptist preached in the wilderness and multitudes from Israel came out to hear him and be baptized. This was a water baptism of repentance for the forgiveness of sins, a precursor to the baptism of the Holy Spirit, which Jesus would introduce on the Day of Pentecost (Mark 1:8).

Another example is when a group of men brought a paralytic to Jesus. They couldn't find a way to get close to Jesus, because of the crowds, so they made a hole in the roof of the house where He was teaching and lowered their friend down to be healed by Jesus. These friends had one purpose in bringing their friend to Jesus: they wanted him to be healed of his paralysis. They had undoubtedly heard of all the miracles Jesus was doing and knew that if they could just get their friend in front of Jesus, he, too, would be healed. When Jesus "saw their faith," He said something rather unusual to the paralytic, leaving everyone in the room either confused or conflicted. Jesus said, "Take heart, son, your sins are forgiven" (Matt. 9:2).

I don't know about you, but if I were that paralytic man, I would have been somewhat perplexed. My thoughts may have been something like this: "People said Jesus could heal me of my physical condition; they made no mention of my sins being discussed at a public church service!" Not only was this man likely confused, the religious leaders were also perturbed, saying to themselves, "Who does this man think he is? God alone can forgive sins." Since Jesus could read their thoughts, He addressed them, the crowd, and the paralytic man, saying, "Which is easier to say, your sins are forgiven, or rise up and walk? But so that you may know that the Son of Man has authority on earth to forgive sins, I say to you, pick up your mat and go home." The paralytic man rose to his feet completely healed. His forgiveness created an uproar in the religious community.

We have too long preached the forgiveness of sins as the culmination of the gospel message, but this can't be true since we see these many examples of forgiveness offered prior to the work of the cross. Some people might argue, using this last example, that because it was Jesus, He was able to forgive sins as God. But that can't be true either because otherwise He would not have had to die on the cross.

All of this leads to a crucial question. If *forgiveness* of sins was offered *before* the cross, then what was the purpose of the cross, the burial, the resurrection, and ascension? What did Jesus accomplish at the cross if people were having their sins forgiven prior to the cross? Let's look at a couple of Scriptures that will shed light on this.

> *"The next day he saw Jesus coming toward him, and said, 'Behold, the Lamb of God, who takes away the sin of the world!'" (John 1:29)*

> *"For since the law has but a shadow of the good things to come instead of the true form of these realities, it can never, by the same sacrifices that are continually offered every year, make perfect those who draw near. Otherwise, would they not have ceased to be offered, since the worshipers, having once been cleansed, would no longer have any consciousness of sins? But in these sacrifices there is a reminder of sins every year. For it is impossible for the blood of bulls and goats to take away sins." (Heb. 10:1-4)*

We see from these passages that the work of the cross does more than offer mankind the forgiveness for their sins; it offers a complete removal of our sinful nature. The blood of Jesus *takes away* not only the sins we have committed, but the nature of sin that made us commit sin in the first place! This is eternal redemption. This is the Good News!

> THE WORK OF THE CROSS OFFERS MANKIND MORE THAN THE FORGIVENESS FOR OUR SINS; IT OFFERS A COMPLETE REMOVAL OF OUR SINFUL NATURE.

A NEW NATURE

He crucified our sinful nature on the cross and became our sin so that we could become His righteousness. The justifying power of God to make our spirit righteous completely changes our very nature. If God's salvation could not meet the deepest need of humanity and if the blood of Jesus was unable to cleanse us from all sin, then His salvation is not as grand as He made it out to be. It minimizes the power of the gospel message to believe you still have a sinful nature. It undermines what He did for us and it leaves us powerless against sin and the desires of the flesh. The gospel is God's power to save us from all sin, and it is only when we start to believe this profound truth that we will experience the freedom it promises.

When we are justified, we receive the righteousness of God as a gift. Our sinful nature is crucified with Christ, and we receive our new nature by the Holy Spirit, as a deposit of the glory that is to come. Once we realize and believe this magnificent truth, we will no longer allow ourselves to identify with the many effects of the fall of man. In good faith we will not use excuses like "Well, I'm only human" to justify sinful behavior. True transformation occurs when we believe and apply the truth of our new nature, allowing our minds to continually be renewed in the fact that the blood of Jesus has not just put us in a positional place of righteousness before God, but He has actually transformed our very nature. It becomes futile to try and walk out the Christian faith. In the revelation of the power of the gospel, we understand who we have become, and can simply be who God has made us to be.

It ultimately comes down to a question of what we believe. The gospel is powerful because it leads us to believe how God sees us. When someone believes the gospel, the fact that they are righteous, it becomes awkward and unnatural to commit a sinful act. Sin feels like an alien behavior, an intrusion to their righteous reign in life.

WHAT DOES THE GOSPEL SAY ABOUT US?

"Long ago, at many times and in many ways, God spoke to our fathers by the prophets, but in these last days He has spoken to us by His Son…" (Heb. 1:1-2)

"Therefore we must pay much closer attention to what we have heard, lest we drift away from it." (Heb. 2:1)

It would be prudent to take a closer look at how God views us and come into agreement with His assessment. What have we heard? We have heard through the life of Jesus that God really loves the world! He has proven His love by sending His Son Jesus to die on a cross. Through this astounding gift, He has also proven how much He values us. He has made a bold declaration to mankind that we are of tremendous value to His heart, so much so that He went to the extreme of sacrificing His Son to destroy the sinful nature that separated us, giving us the righteousness that is required in order to be close to Him.

We know that it is impossible for a sinner to be intimate with a holy God. We instinctively know that if we want to draw close to God, we must be holy as He is holy. Leonard Ravenhill says it this way: "You know people say today, 'Oh, I'm just a saved sinner.' That's like saying you're a married bachelor. That's like saying you're an honest thief or a pure harlot. You can't be a saved sinner. You're either saved or you're a sinner. You know, we live in day when we're more afraid of holiness than we are of sinfulness."

It takes humility to wear the robe of righteousness. He became sin so you could become righteousness. He wasn't too prideful to become our sin, and He calls us to lay down our pride in order to become His righteousness. Wear it confidently, knowing that you will bring much more glory to Him wearing His righteousness than trying to falsely embrace a fallen nature that He crucified 2000 years ago.

IT TAKES HUMILITY TO WEAR THE ROBE OF RIGHTEOUSNESS.

We know that through our union with Christ, our sinful nature has been removed. But the reason many Christians are still struggling with sin is because the gospel they heard promised freedom from sin in their spirit (justification and eternal life) but not freedom from sin in their soul. We have rightly said that if you put your faith in Jesus, you will be reconciled to God and have eternal life. This is the righteousness of God being imputed to our spirits by grace through faith. But without promising complete freedom from sin in our souls (our minds, our wills, and our emotions), we have made sanctification a process of human effort, striving against a sinful nature we no longer have. The harder we try to obey God, the more sanctified we become. The more we read the Bible, go to church, and behave selflessly, the more freedom we will experience in our souls. We have concluded we must still have a sinful nature if we still have a capacity to sin. We have made the mistake of believing that since we are still tempted with carnal, sinful desires that those desires come from our true self. These carnal desires are but remnants in our souls. They are the byproduct of having been "raised" or "tutored" by the defeated mindset inherited through the fall of man. This is why there are so many exhortations in the Word that we be renewed in our minds.

It is through this renewal of our minds that we will experience the transformation that has taken place in our spirits through justification. The believer becomes a new creation, with a new heart and brand-new righteous desires, having had the laws of God etched into his heart by the Holy Spirit. The promise of the gospel is that we are a brand-new creation with a righteous God-given nature that is no longer prone to sin or wander.

OUR DIVINE NATURE

This new nature that we now partake of is a divine nature (2 Peter 1:4) that has been given to us freely according to what Jesus has done on our behalf. It is given to us through the promise of the gospel. We cannot earn the divine nature through righteous living; it is *from* the divine nature that we live righteously. Since the gospel that has been preached and believed has only promised eternal life, most Christians only hope to be free from sin when they die. There is little hope or expectation that we can be free from sin now.

I've heard it said that if we are not truly free from sin until we die, then Jesus isn't our Savior, death is. The new nature that is promised to us is given to us the moment we put our faith in Jesus Christ. The moment someone confesses Jesus Christ as his Lord and Savior, God takes that person, washes him in the blood of Jesus, and then fills him with the precious Holy Spirit. The Holy Spirit is the divine nature that is given to us. Because we are made one with the Lord, we now have the ability, by grace, to walk just like He walked, in perfect righteousness and holiness. We quite literally become one with God through the Holy Spirit: "But whoever is united with the Lord is one with Him in spirit." (1 Cor. 6:17).

In the New Covenant we are born again with a new nature, with the very righteousness of God etched into our hearts, a new and righteous creation. This means that now, under the New Covenant, we have the desire to do what is right! It is in our hearts!

FROM CATS TO DOGS

"Therefore, if anyone is in Christ, he is a new creation. The old has passed away; behold, the new has come." (2 Cor. 5:17)

I love the language in the Bible because it is so clear and so extreme. It leaves no room for doubt, and only when we over-spiritualize its meaning will we miss the weight of what it is trying to say. Let's examine the "new nature" we have access to once we have been born of God through Christ Jesus. To help us understand how completely and powerfully the gospel transforms us, let's imagine that all those who are not saved are cats, though you could easily substitute dogs here if you are a cat lover. Imagine that before you were born again you were a cat. You meowed, you jumped up onto kitchen counters and onto the dining table, and, overall, you were difficult to please. Because you were a cat, it came very naturally for you to act like a cat. You didn't have to try to behave like a cat because you were a cat, so the things that cats do came easily to you.

It is the same thing with someone who has a "sinful nature" or who is a "sinner." Because they have a sinful nature, sinning comes very naturally to them. It is in their nature to make poor decisions, choose wrong behaviors, and hurt people. I think most people who have been born again can relate to a time in their lives when they were "stuck" in their sin; any effort they made to get right failed because they were fighting against their own nature. No matter how hard a cat tries to be a dog, it will fail. A cat doesn't know how to bark or wag its tail because it is not in its nature to do those things. The same is true of a sinner. No matter how hard a sinner tries to do the right thing or walk righteously he will fail, because his nature will eventually take over and reveal what is inside of him. This is why everyone must be born again.

> *"Jesus answered him, 'Truly, truly, I say to you, unless one is born again he cannot see the Kingdom of God.' Nicodemus said to Him, 'How can a man be born when he is old? Can he enter a second time into his mother's womb and be born?' Jesus answered, 'Truly, truly, I say to you, unless one is born of water and the Spirit, he cannot enter the Kingdom of God. That which is born of the flesh is flesh, and that which is born of the Spirit is spirit.'" (John 3:3-6)*

Flesh and blood (or the sinful nature which all of us have been born into) cannot inherit the Kingdom of God. As Paul writes, "I declare to you, brothers and sisters, that flesh and blood cannot inherit the Kingdom of God, nor does the perishable inherit the imperishable" (1 Cor. 15:50).

In these verses we see that in order for an individual to experience and inherit God's Kingdom, he must be born again. To continue the earlier analogy, let's assume that once someone is born again, he is transformed, in a moment, from a cat to a dog. Since our physical bodies do not necessarily immediately change when we give our lives to Christ, we have to understand this analogy on a spiritual level. Our sinful nature (cat) comes underneath the blood of Jesus and the redemption of the cross, and by God's marvelous grace and power, He changes our very nature from sinner to saint, or from cat to dog. Now, instead of having a propensity to sin, we receive Christ's nature, His very righteousness, as a gift. This is justification and is what most people refer to as their conversion. While we were cats, we were unable to bark or act like a dog because we had the nature of a cat. But to carry the analogy on, if we have now been given the nature of a dog, then it will become natural for us to do the things a dog does, if we truly believe that we have a new nature. The problem is that many church leaders and doctrines have told people who are born again that they are still cats. We have told them that they are still prone to wander and thus they continue to manifest the nature of their old lives. But if we are born again and become a "new creature," then that means we have the ability to do things we were unable to do prior to being born again.

> *"For our sake, He made Him to be sin who knew no sin, so that in Him we might become the righteousness of God."* (2 Cor. 5:21)

Your new divine and righteous nature equips and empowers you to live like never before, with peace and freedom and joy. The secret, then, to living out of your new nature is for you to be renewed in your mind. In this way the fruit of the Spirit, which He has planted in you, will be activated in you, by faith, which will enable you to imitate the powerful life of Jesus. If it is true that we have become the righteousness of God, then it will directly affect how we approach God and walk with Him in relationship. If a guilty conscience in relationships stifles intimacy, then a clean conscience must certainly lead to a relationship of passion, love, and friendship.

THE SECRET TO LIVING OUT OF YOUR NEW NATURE IS TO BE RENEWED IN YOUR MIND.

CHAPTER 11
RIGHT STANDING

"Therefore, brothers, since we have confidence to enter the holy places by the blood of Jesus, by the new and living way that he opened for us through the curtain, that is, through his flesh, and since we have a great priest over the house of God, let us draw near with a true heart in full assurance of faith, with our hearts sprinkled clean from an evil conscience and our bodies washed with pure water."

Hebrews 10:19-22

The chief aim, highest goal, and greatest longing of every human heart, since the fall of mankind, is to be right with God and to be free from the guilt and condemnation of our offenses, so that we can enjoy fellowship with Him. Every soul, deep down, wants to stand before God in confidence and know that He accepts us. It drives our behavior and fuels the way we view God.

We instinctively know that because God hates sin, disobedience, and rebellion, the only way to His heart is through perfection. Each person has his or her own way of trying to perfect his or her conscience before God in order to have real, intimate fellowship with the Holy One. The Jewish law was established as a means by which God's people could maintain relationship with Him. But the problem with the law, just as with any other method that we use to connect with God, is that it cannot make us perfect. Perfection is the real issue. It is what we need and long for, as it is the only way we can have an intimate relationship with a holy God. The writer of Hebrews articulates this by saying: "For on the one hand, a former commandment is set aside because of its weakness and uselessness (for the law made nothing perfect); but on the other hand, a better hope is introduced, through which we draw near to God." (Heb. 7:18-19).

The law could merely provide *forgiveness* of sins. But Christ, initiating the New Covenant offered the *removal* of sins, once and for all. If sin is removed, then our conscience is perfected in Him and we have legal, God-given access to be in a free and intimate relationship with Him. If we are continually seeking to have our sins forgiven, instead of understanding that they have been entirely removed, we have failed to understand the foundation on the New Covenant and we will constantly strive against a system of do's and dont's. Hebrews 10:1-2 says, "The law...can never, by the same sacrifices that are continually offered every year, make perfect those who draw near. Otherwise, would they not have ceased to be offered, since the worshippers, having once been cleansed, would no longer have any consciousness of sins?"

In this context, perfection is not having perfect behavior, but having no consciousness of your dead sinful nature that has been crucified and buried with Christ. This perfection of our conscience is the foundation of our New Covenant relationship with the Lord, and our understanding of this concept will directly affect the depth of our intimacy with Him.

The Apostle Paul reiterates this point by saying, "But with me it is a very small thing that I should be judged by you or by any human court. In fact, I do not even judge myself. For I am not aware of anything against myself, but I am not thereby acquitted. It is the Lord who judges me" (1 Cor. 4:3-4). Paul is not saying that his behavior is perfect, but I do think he is speaking of his perfected conscience that he has before the Lord. He acknowledges that he is unaware of anything against himself, meaning that his conscience before the Lord has been perfected. But he goes on to say that, just because his conscience has been perfected, that doesn't mean he is the ultimate judge of himself—that job belongs to the Lord. When you are not aware of your own sinfulness (which we have contended was crucified and buried with Christ), it allows you to remain confident of your right standing with God.

OUR STANDING IN THE NEW COVENANT

Our confusion about where we stand with God often comes from a misunderstanding of the fact that we belong to a New Covenant. We read the Old Testament and derive theologies (beliefs about the nature of God) based on His actions within the confines of an inferior covenant. God was limited in His relationship with the people of Israel because sin had not yet been fully dealt with. The context in which He related to mankind hinged on the systems in place that dealt with the forgiveness of sins. Under the Old Covenant there was not yet provision for the *removal of sin,* so sacrifices and offerings had to be made in order for people to be in right standing with God. To illustrate this point further, Paul says in Galatians 3:23, "Now before faith came, we were held captive under the law." Before faith came, sin reigned in death, and there was no revelation of the righteousness of God that could be attained by faith (Rom. 3:21).

But when Christ came, He initiated the New Covenant and provided a way for all who believed in His name to be justified or made perfect. This covenant will last forever since His life is indestructible and since He is the mediator of this covenant (Heb. 7:16). The New Covenant is established on the basis of our sins and sinful nature being removed once and for all. When, as New Testament believers, we operate under the regulations of the Old Testament, an inferior covenant, we cut ourselves off from the glory of Christ's sacrifice and remove ourselves from the position of grace that Jesus paid such a high price for. Our conscience becomes defiled through examining our life and behavior through the lens of the law, rather than the lens of grace, which ultimately leads us to dead works. These dead works are a result of a defiled conscience trying to make amends and payment for "not measuring up" to God's righteous standards.

THE NEW COVENANT IS ESTABLISHED ON THE BASIS OF THE REMOVAL OF OUR SINS AND SINFUL NATURE ONCE AND FOR ALL.

I often counsel believers who are struggling with a sin habit. One of the most common struggles I find is lust and sexual addiction. Guys (and girls) will confess that they are stuck in a habit of looking at pornography and don't know what to do to get free. Those that come to me are often plagued by a tremendous sense of guilt and shame because they truly have a desire to walk in righteousness but find themselves stuck in this painful cycle. Inevitably the repeated "failure" or "stumbling" into this sin habit begins to defile their conscience, and they are tempted to believe that something must in fact be wrong with them. This feeling of inadequacy or the consciousness of sin within almost always leads the person to try and *do* something to get free. They come to me in humility and brokenness over sin, truly repentant, and all they want to know is what to *do*. Because they feel guilty before God, they feel the need to make up for their mistakes, typically through some rigorous spiritual discipline. The problem with this approach is that it leads to dead works and ultimately stems from a deception that is brought about through the sin habit. We will look in depth in later chapters at breaking free from a sin habit, but for now we must understand that the blood of Jesus cleanses our conscience thoroughly from sins.

A GUILTY OR PURE CONSCIENCE

We must also understand that there is a direct link between the inward state of our conscience and our external behavior (Heb. 9:14). If our conscience is evil, we will naturally operate in dead works. If our conscience is pure and perfect, it will enable us to approach God without fear so that we may receive mercy in our time of need (Heb. 9 and 10). As John Calvin said, "The torture of a bad conscience is the hell of a living soul."

For this reason, those with the guiltiest of consciences go one of two ways. Either they deny the existence of God because they cannot bear the constant shame and angst of not measuring up, or they end up thrusting themselves into Christian service and activities, trying to appease their conscience through works. Either path results in a constant sense of anguish and shame for not "measuring up." Choosing the "moral" way will lead you to a legalistic life of striving in spiritual activity plagued with a guilty conscience. In vain, we cannot hope that the more "work" we do for God, the cleaner our conscience will become. Sadly, pulpits and pews are filled with such souls who have never known or experienced the ecstasy of having their conscience cleansed by the blood and liberated from an awareness of internal sin. The end of this path leads to being burned out or depressed because, no matter how sincerely and genuinely you try to cleanse your conscience through Christian activity, you will fail. The only remedy is to believe that the blood of Jesus truly cleanses you and intends to take away any consciousness you have of sin in your inmost being.

The other extreme path leads to atheism or the denial of God's existence. Their conscience being unable to bear up under the daily belief that they are failing the standard and approval of a God in heaven, they convince themselves there is no god. This is why it is not uncommon for someone to grow up in the church but end up as an atheist. Being exposed to the supposed conditional love and acceptance of God expressed through good behavior, church attendance, and a pious life, they come to believe in and eventually reject a "god" who has been made in the image of these religious institutions. This is one of the many woes of the Church abandoning the simplicity and purity of the gospel. But by God's grace, we are coming back to the gospel, learning and believing that His blood does speak a better word and has the power to cleanse us in our inmost being from all consciousness of sin.

CHAPTER 12
SANCTIFICATION THROUGH INTIMACY

"The best thing of all is God is with us."

John Wesley

After justification, the second aspect of the work of Christ in our salvation is His present life, sanctifying our soul. And we know from the Scriptures that Jesus, having been resurrected, is alive and is seated at the right hand of the Father. We know that Jesus is interceding for us:

> *"Who is to condemn? Christ Jesus is the one who died—more than that, who was raised—who is at the right hand of God, who indeed is interceding for us." (Rom. 8:34)*

We know that if we sin, He is our Advocate to the Father:

> *"My little children, I am writing these things to you so that you may not sin. But if anyone does sin, we have an advocate with the Father, Jesus Christ the righteous." (1 John 2:1)*

This Jesus who is alive has become our sanctification:

> *"And because of Him you are in Christ Jesus, who became to us wisdom from God, righteousness and sanctification and redemption." (1 Cor. 1:30)*

So we see that our sanctification is not so much a work that we must perform, but a simple faith in the One who been raised and seated at the right hand of God. Our faith in the Living Jesus is what allows us to have a relationship with Him, hearing His voice and becoming more intimately aware of the nature of the One Whose image we've been given. If we as the Church do not dare to believe that we can walk with and know the resurrected Jesus, then we will be given no access to this grace of sanctification. We cannot preach the work of Christ that leads to justification and then expect the people of God to receive the grace of sanctification unless we equip them in this powerful truth. The work of Christ was specific and thorough, and we as ministers and stewards of the mysteries of God must preach and declare the whole counsel of God in order that the people of God may enter into the fullness of salvation.

Sanctification results in the mind, will, and emotions of Jesus becoming our very own. While most people agree that sanctification is a "process" stemming from the finished work of the cross, I would like to present a slightly different process than what has been taught in the church. The reason for this clarification is because I believe many believers who are struggling with sin and leading passionless and joyless Christian lives do so because of a poor understanding of their sanctification. They have been taught that their sanctification hinges on their ability to obey or cultivate certain spiritual disciplines. Without understanding the strength of our justification, many people are trying to put to death the desires of the flesh in their own strength through self-discipline. This has led to "performance Christianity," where believers are measured to be more mature or spiritual based on the self-control they exhibit over their fleshly desires. The process of sanctification in these Christian circles then becomes one that hinges on the sincerity and strength of the individual to control their sinful habits through spiritual disciplines such as accountability groups, going to church, and other spiritual activities. These disciplines in themselves are obviously not the problem—it is when someone relies upon these things for their justification or sanctification that the true growth into the nature and likeness of Christ is stunted.

> THROUGH SANCTIFICATION, THE MIND, WILL, AND EMOTIONS OF JESUS BECOME OUR VERY OWN.

This man-made "process of sanctification" is endemic in the Body of Christ and must be addressed if we want to see the Church mature into her glorious identity as the pure and spotless Bride of Christ. Instead of relying upon spiritual disciplines for sanctification, I would like to define sanctification as the following:

> *True Christian sanctification takes place in this life through intimacy with Christ. If the Christian was justified and born of God through the death, burial and resurrection of Christ, then the Christian is sanctified by enjoying fellowship and intimacy with the Living Christ.*

The results of experiencing a true sanctifying grace offered through the gospel is a life that is marked by holiness, dominion over sin, and a living and vibrant relationship with the Lord. As we yield to this grace offered by our Resurrected King, we will find that our thoughts, feelings, and actions begin to more clearly mirror those of Jesus. To reiterate this truth in light of the struggle so many are having with sexual addiction, sanctification and freedom from this sin comes about by discovering the beauty of God, falling in love with Him through the Holy Spirit, and enjoying the pleasure of knowing Him, which far surpasses the temporal pleasure that sexual sin brings. However, those who seek to overcome this struggle through their own effort or human wisdom will find themselves defeated in shame and feeling like a substandard Christian for not being able to break free.

LOVE LEADS TO OBEDIENCE

Because of these great promises of salvation, life as a New Testament believer should be exciting. Believers should be the most optimistic, hope-filled, joy-filled, peaceful, and triumphant people on the earth. The source of this distinction comes from the freedom produced by our radical love affair with the Creator of the Universe. However, much of the Church is unaware of the reality of this level of intimacy they can have with God. We can talk about relationship, but few actually live it out.

Before He is crucified, Jesus is encouraging His disciples in John 14:15, "If you love me, you will keep my commandments." Many have read this to mean that if we disobey God, we must not love Him. We have assumed our love for Jesus is contingent upon our obedience, but I don't believe that is what Jesus is saying. I believe He is declaring that when we are radically in love with Him, we will be supernaturally empowered by grace to keep and obey all His commandments. In our love for Him, we will long to do the things that please Him and what used to feel like a burden will become a delight. In the realm of love, obedience becomes a delight and stems from our heart. This is why our relational connection and intimacy with the Lord is so important and why we must have a strong biblical foundation to give us confidence and hope that this type of intimacy is possible.

The misunderstanding of this Scripture has led to a joyless, powerless, and discouraged Bride of Christ. The remedy for this is love. Fall in love with God, and you will say along with the Psalmist, "I delight to do your will, O my God, your law is within my heart" (Psalm 40:8).

THE FRUIT OF SANCTIFICATION

Now that we have established that growth and maturity in God happens through intimacy, how do we experience this salvation in our soul, and why do I keep struggling with sin? To experience salvation in our soul, we must be delivered from the power of sin, which is the law. We have already established that God's salvation is experienced by the impartation of His righteousness to our spirit, soul, and body, received by grace through faith. Thus, when we daily put our faith in Jesus Christ, the person of Holy Spirit comes into our mind, will and emotions and makes them all righteous.

He makes our mind like His mind...

> *"But we have the mind of Christ." (1 Cor. 2:16)*

He makes our emotions like His…

> *"For God is my witness, how I long for you all with the affection of Christ Jesus." (Phil. 1:8)*
>
> *"I am speaking the truth in Christ—I am not lying; my conscience bears me witness in the Holy Spirit—that I have great sorrow and unceasing anguish in my heart. For I could wish that I myself were accursed and cut off from Christ for the sake of my brothers, my kinsmen according to the flesh." (Rom. 9:1-3)*

He even makes our will like His…

> *"'Behold, I have come to do your will.' He does away with the first in order to establish the second. And by that will we have been sanctified through the offering of the body of Jesus Christ once for all." (Heb. 10:9-10)*
>
> *"But thanks be to God, that you who were once slaves of sin have become obedient from the heart…" (Rom. 6:17)*

We see that in every aspect of life God intends to make our mind, emotions, and will like the very mind, emotions, and will of Jesus. This transformation requires the power of God (His grace) to manifest in each area of our life. This manifest transformative power can be experienced in our soul through simple belief. If we believe we have received this salvation in our soul, it would be absolutely futile to place any sort of regulations or law for righteous living on ourselves or other Christians. To do so would be contrary to what we say we believe—that we have already become the righteousness of God and have the mind, will, and emotions of Jesus!

Our exhortation therefore for those who are still babies in Christ is to equip and empower them in their relationship with God. We must help establish people in the New Covenant so that, through their intimacy with Christ, they will grow up and mature out of sinful habits and into the beauty of the life of Christ.

RENEW THE MIND

One of my favorite things to do in a church is to help people see how brand-new the gospel has made them. It is when we realize just how powerful the gospel is in our life that we will be able to walk out our Christian faith effortlessly. This effortless faith walk comes about through a thorough and radical transformation of the mind, as Paul writes: "Do not be conformed to this world, but be transformed by the renewal of your mind" (Rom. 12:2).

WHEN WE REALIZE JUST HOW POWERFUL THE GOSPEL IS IN OUR LIFE, WE WILL BE ABLE TO WALK OUT OUR CHRISTIAN FAITH EFFORTLESSLY.

I have found that the result of having a renewed mind is an effortless faith walk, while the actual effort it takes to have our minds renewed is a process that takes great intentionality. So our effort and discipline is rightly placed when it is focused on the renewal of the mind and not behavior modification. This renewal of the mind takes place by the Holy Spirit, but we have a choice whether or not we want to believe the word of God. If I sit on my couch and eat Oreos all day and watch SportsCenter for an entire week, I will have no greater consciousness of God than the week before. My mind will not be further renewed. However, if I choose to wake up each morning and spend a couple of hours in the Word of God, thanking God for His promises that are true and spending time meditating on and receiving these truths, my mind will be renewed. By God's grace, I will have a greater consciousness and awareness of God than I did the week before. To renew our minds, there is time and effort involved, but it is worth every ounce of energy we spend.

RIGHTEOUSNESS IS A GIFT

In regards to the renewing of the mind, one of the most important truths is understanding that righteousness is a gift of God. I believe one of God's greatest desires is for us to believe that our identity and nature are now like Jesus and no longer like the sinner and pauper so many have long identified as.

The reason this is so important is because it has often been taught that we as Christians have a dual nature. The conclusion is that since we retain the capacity to sin, we must still have a sinful nature that is warring against God's imputed righteousness. The belief is that since the majority of Christians seem to still be bound in sinful habits, there must be a sinful nature at work within each of us. If Christians are convinced that they still have a sinful nature, it should be no surprise when they constantly struggle with sin. Because they believe they are sinful, they manifest sin. And because they manifest sin, it becomes necessary for church leaders to address, manage, and control these sinful behaviors through programs, accountability, and church discipline. The underlying belief amongst believers and in many churches is that the more spiritually disciplined you are, the more people you have around you, and the greater the accountability you have, the more freedom you will experience. They begin to quantify spiritual maturity and freedom by how much control one has over their carnal desires. Their right standing with God hinges on the spiritual disciplines, accountability, and fellowship. People are taught that the more consistent, faithful, and wholehearted you are, the more you will be made righteous. This legalistic church mindset is reminiscent to what Paul found in the Galatian church: "Are you so foolish? Having begun in the spirit, are you now being perfected by the flesh?" (Gal. 3:3).

If we advocate that our entrance into the Kingdom and birth into the New Covenant is received by grace through faith and that nothing can take away the promise of eternal life, we must also wholeheartedly subscribe to the belief that our growth and maturity happens the same way. The Bible addresses this point with some very strong language.

If you have been taught that your righteousness is contingent on your spiritual discipline, then you have been deceived. If you have believed that, since you struggle with sin after becoming a believer, you are "less" righteous in any way, then you have been deceived. The Christian that continues to struggle (I repeat, struggle) with sin is no less righteous than the brother or sister who has perfectly lived in piety and purity for 20 years. Why? Because the righteousness of God is a gift given to us by God. It is not a position we can earn or achieve. If we could overcome sin merely through spiritual discipline, then Christ died for no reason. It is through faith that one experiences the manifestation of God's righteousness in their actual thoughts and behavior.

CHAPTER 13

LAW AND GRACE

"For sin will have no dominion over you, since you are not under law but under grace."

Romans 6:14

Let's address the question that most people have in light of the gospel's power to completely save their soul, completely remove their sin nature, make them righteous, and give them the very nature of God. *If this is true, why do I keep struggling with sin?* One of the main reasons may be that no one has ever presented the gospel to you in such a way that gave you permission to be free from it. You have never believed it is possible to be free, so you continue to struggle.

Let us be clear on how everyone is wired. What we believe directly affects how we feel, and how we feel affects how we behave. If we do not believe it is possible to be free from sin, then we will never actually feel free from sin, and therefore we will always continue to sin. But if we are renewed in the spirit of our minds and believe the gospel that promises every believer a brand-new, righteous nature, then we will start to feel like we truly have been made clean and righteous. And when we feel righteous, we will effortlessly manifest righteousness in all that we say and do.

So the first thing we must do in the midst of a sin struggle is to believe it is possible to be free from the power of sin based on the finished work of the cross. Hold yourself accountable to believe rightly, for it is from your belief that your feelings about your new nature and righteous behavior will follow.

> THE FIRST THING WE NEED TO DO WHEN WE ARE STRUGGLING WITH SIN IS TO BELIEVE IT IS POSSIBLE TO BE FREE FROM THE POWER OF SIN THROUGH THE FINISHED WORK OF THE CROSS.

STRUGGLING WITH SIN

Let me explain how I discern whether or not someone is "struggling" with sin. There are instances in the Bible where we find people within a church fellowship who are living in sin but not struggling against it. A Biblical example that comes to mind is the man in the Corinthian church who is sleeping with his mother-in-law and boasting about it at church (1 Cor. 5:1-2). Paul strongly warns the Corinthians that this man will corrupt the entire body if they don't break fellowship with him and warn him that his actions will certainly lead to death. So when I say someone is struggling with sin, I am not referring to people who want to make a law of grace to justify their sinful behavior. Their rebellion is a mockery to the cross and should be confronted. In love, clear boundaries should be communicated so their deceived mindset does not spread throughout the body of believers.

But the reality that I have seen since being in ministry is that most Christians I interact with do not fall in this category. The brothers or sisters that I know who are struggling with sin are genuinely grieved and want nothing more than to be free from their sin habit. They know it's wrong but are unaware of the power they have through the Holy Spirit to overcome it. These are the people my heart bleeds for, because most of the ones that I've talked to have been given prescriptions from the church on how to manage their sin, instead of being shown the gospel, which sets them free from the power of sin.

If we tell someone who is struggling in a certain sin habit that their righteousness or freedom can be attained if they read the Bible, spend time with God every day, or plug into an accountability group or program, then what happens when they do all the prescriptions but continue to struggle with sin? Like I did, most people will start questioning whether or not they did those activities properly. *Well, maybe I didn't spend enough time with God? Maybe instead of 30 minutes each morning I should bump it up to an hour, and then God will give me the strength to overcome this sin. Maybe I should confess to my pastor as well, not just to the accountability group. Maybe I should read that self-help book that was recommended. Maybe I should try going on a mission trip and getting out of this rut.*

The list is never ending, and you will find yourself in an exhausting cycle that only leads to more discouragement and sin. When good things become laws that must be followed in the attempt to achieve freedom, you will only know defeat. Freedom from sin is only available in the realm of grace.

LAW IS THE POWER OF SIN

If we do not have a sinful nature, then why do sinful desires still have power over my decision-making? To answer this, I want to clearly establish that the power of sin at work in the life of believers lies not within our nature but in the law.

As Paul writes, "The sting of death is sin, and the power of sin is the law" (1 Cor. 15:56). It is only the sanctifying grace of God experienced through intimacy that removes us from the power of the law and enables us to live out our new God-given nature, which will in fact enable us to walk free from all sinful habits.

The Bible is explicit in showing us that the reason sin has power over a believer's life is because of the law. It does not say that the power of sin is our sinful nature. It does not say that sin's power lies within our wicked heart. It says that the power of sin is in the law. We are deceived if we think applying a list of spiritual principles will actually help manage our behavior. This will actually further manifest the sin in our life, because inevitably these spiritual principles applied become a law or measuring stick of our righteousness.

In the same way that we are convinced that we believe we are going to heaven regardless of what happens in life because we have committed our life to Jesus, we must also advocate that no matter what sin struggle we find ourselves in, we remain in righteous standing as sons and daughters of God because of what Christ has done. Paul argues this bluntly in Romans: "Apart from the law, sin lies dead" (Rom. 7:8).

We must remove the demands and laws we have placed on ourselves and others to achieve freedom, and simply adopt the gospel in such a way that gives us all permission to be dead to sin and alive to God. We must live in light of what Paul says in Romans 6: "For sin will have no dominion over you, since you are not under law but under grace" (Rom. 6:14).

If someone is *struggling* with and against a sin habit, it is because they are born again and have a new righteous nature that is now uncomfortable with their sin. Before we were saved, we could partake of sinful activities without feeling much more than perhaps a worldly sense of guilt. But now that we are righteous children of God, we wake up every morning with a desire to walk righteously. Because the law of God is written on our hearts, we have a genuine desire to please Him and walk in obedience. I don't believe that in Christ "we are prone to wander" like the old hymn says. I believe we are now, in Christ, prone to follow Him, walk in righteousness, and serve Him faithfully. So instead of shaming and condemning a Christian brother that is stuck in some habit, we must help them see and believe the gospel. It is the power of God to save to the uttermost, reminding us that, no matter what we've done and no matter what we do, we have received God's righteousness as a gift by the blood of Jesus. The reason we as believers are tormented over sin is because we have God living inside of us. He is never going to leave, forsake, or shame us because of our sin struggle, setting an example for us to not leave or shame others who are struggling with sin. God so desired to demonstrate His love for us that while we were still sinning, He died for us. This means He is not afraid of our sin and that He is not ashamed of us if we sin. On the contrary, He runs toward us to meet us in our sin and provides the way back to a free and intimate relationship with Him, which will ultimately lead to freedom from sin.

AS BELIEVERS, THE REASON WE ARE TORMENTED OVER SIN IS BECAUSE WE HAVE GOD LIVING INSIDE OF US.

AN ENVIRONMENT OF GRACE

"For sin will have no dominion over you because you are not under law but under grace." (Rom. 6:14)

As the law arouses our sinful nature, so our righteous nature is aroused by grace. It is only in an environment of grace that our righteous nature can function and thrive. If someone believes that they are the righteousness of God yet is still trying to be made perfect through spiritual laws and disciplines, then they will continually struggle under the power of sin.

Romans 5:17 puts it perfectly: "For if, because of one man's trespass, death reigned through that one man, much more will those who receive the abundance of grace and the free gift of righteousness reign in life through the one man Jesus Christ."

Through Adam's sin, death began its reign over mankind. Through Jesus Christ, we receive the free gift of righteousness and an abundance of grace (the atmosphere conducive for our righteousness) so that we may now reign in life!

It is not intuitive, but the most righteous, holy behavior will only manifest in an environment of abundant grace. In grace, we must allow people to be who God says they are (righteous) and hold them accountable to their new righteous nature. The moment we define righteous living through a list of do's and don'ts, we empower sin. This is why 1 Corinthians 15:56 says, "The sting of death is sin, and the power of sin is the law."

The power of sin lies within the demands of the law. In Christ, God has removed the demands of the law upon our lives. He has established us in grace and given us access, freedom, and power through the Holy Spirit to live righteously before Him. When we start demanding (law) what the gospel freely promises, we undermine the very power of God to transform an individual. The Church is so accustomed to directing, controlling, and modifying sinful behaviors that we have lost sight of what the gospel truly accomplishes. The gospel is the power of God to save people! If people are still being afflicted by sin, sickness, and disease, then we must go back to the gospel.

> NO ONE WILL EXPERIENCE FREEDOM FROM SIN BY IDENTIFYING WITH THEIR SINFUL NATURE.

If we find ourselves constantly trying to help people who are struggling in sin but do not immediately direct them to the power of the gospel, we will find ourselves fighting a battle we cannot win that exhausts everyone involved. My friend calls it "Christian necromancy." Necromancy is defined as a method of divination through communication with the dead. We bring our old sinful nature from the grave to counsel it, talk to it, manage it, and encourage it to not sin again. No one will experience freedom from sin by identifying with their sinful nature. We must learn to accept and receive the gift of righteousness and perfect nature that God has given us by the Holy Spirit. Listen to these words from Paul:

> *"I have been crucified with Christ. It is no longer I who live, but Christ who lives in me. And the life I now live in the flesh I live by faith in the Son of God, who loved me and gave Himself for me. I do not nullify the grace of God, for if righteousness were through the law, then Christ died for no purpose." (Gal. 2:20-21)*

Paul considered that he himself died with Christ and that the life he lived in the flesh was no longer his own. He lived that life by faith in the Son of God.

Our life and our new identity is found only in Christ. As Christians, we must learn to help each other understand and embrace our God-given righteousness, our new nature. If we can help people see that through the gospel the old sinful nature has been crucified at the cross, then their minds will be renewed by the Holy Spirit, empowering them to put on the new nature that was created in God's own likeness. Once a believer starts to renew their mind as to who they have become in Christ, they will effortlessly manifest the righteousness of God, and old sin habits and struggles will die.

GOVERNED BY GOD'S GRACE IN RELATIONSHIP

We must choose to stop relating to God on a system of do's and don'ts. God tells us that the new nature that He gave us through the Holy Spirit has desires that are opposed to the flesh and that, if we learn to identify ourselves with the Spirit and His desires, we will not gratify the desires of our flesh. In fact, he goes so far as to say that the one who is led by the Spirit is no longer under the law:

> *"But I say, walk by the Spirit, and you will not gratify the desires of the flesh. For the desires of the flesh are against the Spirit, and the desires of the Spirit are against the flesh, for these are opposed to each other, to keep you from doing the things you want to do. But if you are led by the Spirit, you are not under the law." (Gal. 5:16-18)*

However, the reality is that the process of having our minds renewed with this truth will take some time. It will take time in the word of God and communion with the Holy Spirit. And along the way we might mess up and sin. In fact, some people may be stuck in a sin habit that seems impossible to break. Fear is a common sin struggle and one that plagued me since I was a boy. I was afraid of what people thought about me, and that caused me to be shy, quiet, and introverted in a way that hindered me from having healthy friendships. Fear is such a common struggle that many of us believe it is something we will always live with.

One day, God challenged this fear of mine by asking me to talk to a group of strangers about the love of God. I resisted His voice, discounting it as my own imagination. However, the voice persisted, and I felt compelled by God to act. I asked God for some help, a verse, or something that would help me overcome this fear of man. I immediately thought of Proverbs 28:1, which says, "The wicked man flees though no one pursues, but the righteous are as bold as a lion." God was showing me that I was a lion in His eyes and, if I would act like it, this fear that was hounding me would be broken off. I stepped out in faith, still feeling scared, and told this group of strangers that I was riding a public train with that God loved them tremendously and

He longed to have a relationship with each one of them. As I began to believe that God had indeed made me as bold as a lion (my mind being renewed), I could feel the fear of what people thought of me begin to fade away. As I stewarded this belief by reminding myself it was true and acting as if it was true, the fear of man was broken off of my life, and boldness became a new normal.

If a believer is stuck in fear, then the first thing we must do is give them hope that it is possible to be free from those chains that bind them. Believe it or not, as simple as this step may seem, it is not intuitive. It actually contradicts what many people have heard. In fact, I know many people believe that an alcoholic is always an alcoholic and that if they have one sip they will fall back into an old habit. This is rubbish that contradicts every promise of complete freedom found in the word of God. Sin cannot operate with any power in the realm of grace, because grace governs the sons and daughters of God. As Paul writes, "For sin will have no dominion over you, since you are not under law but under grace" (Rom. 6:14).

If someone is only righteous when they are walking righteously, then their righteousness is still based on the law. Scripturally, we can conclude that believers that are stuck in some sinful habit are still relating to God under the law. They still believe that the foundation of their relationship with God is in what they do or don't do. But the promise of the gospel is that we can be righteous, even in the midst of a sin habit, simply because we believe the gospel. In fact, it is believing the gospel that will set one free from the power of any sin. Nowhere in the gospel does it require that we clean up our own selves; therefore, we should not require this from others. It is for freedom that Christ set us free. Our freedom cost Jesus everything, and all we have to do is receive, by faith, what He paid for.

Again, if this is true, then we have to renew our minds and update our tactics in dealing with our own sin and the sins of others. Knowing that we have a new nature that God intended to be governed by grace, all of our strategies and beliefs rooted in an Old Covenant understanding must give way to the truth found in the gospel.

CHAPTER 14
DEALING WITH SIN

"But if anyone does sin, we have an advocate with the Father, Jesus Christ the righteous."

1 John 2:1

In light of the revelation that we have become the righteousness of God in Christ Jesus and are no longer under the law, I wish to address the Biblical response for born-again Christians who do continue to sin in one way or another. I believe confession and repentance are still a necessary and powerful practice in the life of a believer.

As we have established in the previous chapters, if a believer is stuck in sin, they need the hope of freedom. They need to know that Jesus is not angry with them about their sin; He is advocating for them to the Father in the midst of their struggle (see 1 John 2:1). And in the midst of their sin struggle, they need to learn to identify with their God-given nature that is pure and holy. They must continue to believe that in spite of their behavior, they still have a new nature. If we don't believe that we are righteous because of a sin habit, then we are still relating to God through the law and will only continue in our sinful habit.

CONFESSION

Confession within the New Covenant is just like confession in a perfect marriage covenant. Our confession to God does not affect our standing with Him as much as it affects our intimacy with Him. God has purposed in His heart to love us intentionally and unconditionally, whether we sin against Him or not. He does not become offended, throw a fit, and distance Himself from us. God has already proven His love for us that while we were sinning, He died for us (Rom. 5:8). Our confession to God then is a way in which we cultivate intimacy with Him. We know that He will always extend His forgiveness, no matter how many times we sin against Him (1 John 1:9). This means that our confession of sin to God should draw us close to Him as we in humility allow Him to wash us in His grace and kindness.

> CONFESSING SINS TO GOD IS A WAY WE CULTIVATE INTIMACY WITH HIM.

Forgiveness is a relational act that fuels intimacy. I've heard some people say that because they know God will forgive them they don't need to confess their sins anymore; Jesus already forgives them. I don't like that because forgiveness of sins is a relational exchange. If I sin against my wife and move on, assuming that, because she is so kind and forgiving, she will forgive me, I have usurped her right as my wife to offer me forgiveness.

If I sin, I always confess it to God and ask Him to forgive me. I'm not asking Him to renew our covenant, and I'm not questioning my salvation—I am simply allowing my Father to again apply the grace and mercy that He has promised to give me. This always brings me closer to Him and allows Him to speak into that area of my life. He often teaches me why I gave into a carnal desire and gives me wisdom to avoid stumbling in the future.

I also believe in the importance of confessing our sins to other believers. I think one of the devil's most dangerous schemes is to keep our failures in the dark. If we bring our areas of weakness and incidents of sin into the light with those we love, we expose the work of the enemy and remove the power of shame and darkness that attempts to torment us. When our spouse, friend, or pastor speaks truth to us in response to the confession of our struggle, we also are encouraged in the renewing of our mind and edified in our spirit.

Along with confession, I believe another word that is somewhat taboo in some circles is repentance. For too long, I believed that repentance meant I was to feel bad about my sin to the point of humiliation. I thought that the more devastated over my sin and sorry I was to God, the more effective my repentance. But this is not the Biblical definition of repentance! The biblical word for repentance is *metanoeó,* which means to repent, change my mind, or change the inner man (particularly with reference to acceptance of the will of God).

Repentance actually means to change our mind or to change the inner man as it relates to the will of God! What is the will of God you may ask? It is to make every single human being as righteous and as pure as Jesus Christ so that He can have fellowship and intimacy with His creation. This is God's gift, so that no one can boast of their own achievement. Everyone is made righteous the same way—through faith in Jesus Christ.

To help people repent, we must help them change their mind about themselves. We must help them renew their mind to the way that God sees them and relates to them now that they are in the family of God. When your sin lies to you and tells you that you are a sinner, repentance means renouncing that lie, identifying with the divine nature, proclaiming your righteous identity, and believing that your sinful nature has been completely removed. Paul describes this process in Ephesians:

> *"To put off your old self, which belongs to your former manner of life and is corrupt through deceitful desires, and to be renewed in the spirit of your minds, and to put on the new self, created after the likeness of God in true righteousness and holiness." (Eph. 4:22-24)*

Here we see that the Biblical exhortation to a group of believers struggling with sin is to do three things:

1. Put off your old self.
2. Be renewed in the spirit of your mind.
3. Put on the new self.

Because we have been justified, made righteous by the blood of Jesus, we now have practical instruction and God-given power to simply put off any sinful behavior, allow the Spirit of God to renew our minds with just how righteous we have become in Christ, and take a step of faith into that new self which is "created after the likeness of God in true righteousness and holiness." This is repentance. Feeling bad about sin is a given for those who are in relationship with God and are wanting to be free. A true believer will always have a godly sorrow over sin which will lead to true repentance. And true repentance is not just a change in mind but a change in action as well. It is through putting off the old self and renewing our minds to the truth of what we've been born into that we can take bold and powerful steps of faith into a righteous and holy lifestyle!

MAINTAINING FAITH IN THE MIDST OF SIN

This process of repenting and stepping into our sanctification is only possible in an environment of grace, through faith. Indeed, this is always how salvation takes place: "For it is by grace you have been saved, through faith" (Eph. 2:8).

We must learn to encourage and keep our self and others in a place of faith if there is a struggle with sin. Maintaining faith in the midst of a sin struggle is a challenge, but one that is foundational to our soul's sanctification and freedom.

When I was in college, I had an uncontrollable pornography addiction. Although I looked at pornography multiple times a week, I was known by others as the good Christian kid who had everything together. I didn't sleep around with girls or go out partying with the rest of my friends. I was certainly a Christian, but I was living in unbelief, which produced sin in my life. My sin cycle continued for years, resulting in my soul's decay and death. The effects of this sin were so bad that one Christmas break when I went home to visit my family, my mom noticed something was not right. She asked me multiple times if I was okay or if I was feeling sick. I dismissed her inquiries and pretended as if nothing was wrong, but inside a deadly spiritual cancer of guilt, shame, and condemnation was eating away at my consciousness and estranging me from God. I was numb to His love, blind to His power, and disbelieving that His kindness could actually be extended to me. I convinced myself that it was my responsibility to try and climb out of this pit that I had gotten myself into. I remember going to the mirror and looking into my own eyes, something I rarely did. I didn't see a lot of hope. This began a turning point in my pleas to God.

Instead of begging Him to help me not lust, I began to pray prayers such as, *God if you are so strong and mighty to save, why does this thing dominate my life? You are either big enough to handle me in all of my sin or you are not...I want to be able to come to you in this mess, and not feel alone.* After a series of prayers like these, I made a determination in my heart that could have only come from the Spirit of God. He prompted me to immediately go to Him by the blood of Jesus for deliverance and help, no matter how many times I screwed up and looked at pornography. At my heart's core I did not want to keep on sinning. I sincerely desired complete deliverance, and I finally realized the only thing that was going to rescue me was the supernatural love and salvation of God by His Spirit.

Before I had this revelation, I remember I would wait a few days before I came to God, believing that He was angry or frustrated with me for screwing up *again*. I thought I needed to let the dust of His anger settle before I approached Him again. I genuinely believed that when I looked at pornography there was anger in the heart of God towards me. Unknowingly I was living in unbelief, the worst of sins, a breeding ground for demonic spirits of guilt, shame, and condemnation to thrive. Unbelief in what, you may be wondering. Unbelief in the love of God demonstrated to me in remarkable fashion by the Son of God hanging on a cross *for me* and manifest *in me* by the inhabitation of the Holy Spirit. Though my prayers surrounded the issue I had with lust, God had a greater agenda to ultimately deliver me from the very thing that was producing all sin behaviors in my life—unbelief in the simple, but radical power of the gospel.

Instead of waiting a couple of days to approach God, I determined that I would go to Him at the height of my sin and allow His perfect, beautiful light to search me and know me. This took a tremendous amount of humility on my part because everything inside of me wanted to stay in a place of guilt, shame, and condemnation. Those feelings were in a strange way more comfortable, helping me feel as if I was paying for my sin in some way. Distancing myself from God made me feel like I was getting what I deserved and that once the appropriate amount of penance was served, I would eventually be back in good graces with the Lord. Little did I know that the Bible calls that a "dead work" (Heb. 6:1) and that my conscience was actually acting in wickedness. What an insult to the cross of Christ! How could my self-deprecating thoughts and behavior honor the One who paid such a high price to deliver me from that entire manner of hellish thinking?

The first time I did this it felt as unnatural as riding a bike for the first time. I remember looking at pornography and in the very next moment dropping to my knees and saying in faith, *God, here I am! See me! I am your son, and I hate this behavior, but it is dominating my life, and I need your help. I know you love me and will help me out of this pit.* That night was the beginning of a powerful lesson that I believe will set anyone free from the power of sin. I learned that the first thing sin does to a believer is deceive them. Please note I said it is the first thing it does, not the last! As I mentioned before, sin is never taken lightly in the Bible, and it will most emphatically, when full grown, lead to death. But before it becomes full grown, it will first attempt to deceive and blind us to the only remedy that can save us from its gripping power.

As I persisted in the grace of God and refused to let my repeated failures separate me from talking and connecting with God on a relational level, I found His power began to work on my behalf until one day He severed the addiction from my life permanently. It took months of standing in the reality that my righteousness was a gift from God that gave me access to His affection and favor even moments after I sinned, but I encountered His love in such a real, tangible way that set me free and has kept me free for more than ten years.

DON'T LET SIN HARDEN YOUR HEART

"But encourage one another daily, as long as it is called 'today,' so that none of you may be hardened by the deceitful of sin." (Heb. 3:13)

Notice how these verses describe sin as deceitful, ultimately hardening our hearts to the gospel. So the challenge for a believer who is struggling with some sin habit is first to not be hardened by sin's deceit. Sin lies to us and tells us that God doesn't love us in our sin, thus distancing us from the One that can actually free us and give us life.

These truths apply to the one who feels stuck in their sin, in bondage to something that they desperately want to be free from. I have such a heart of compassion and love for anyone facing the despair and desperation of a habitual sin cycle because that is exactly where I was until, by the grace of God, He set me completely free. I want to reiterate that there are some people who are not resisting sin. Because they have been deceived, they are not broken over their sinful choices, and therefore willfully continue to sin. Appealing to the righteousness within them feels futile, because their conscience has become numb and their heart has become hard to the Holy Spirit within them convicting them to repent. Where those desiring righteousness feel miserable over their struggle, we must pray for the hardened to become miserable in their sin and hunger again for the fellowship and peace that comes from an intimate relationship with the Lord. If we truly believe it's true that God's kindness leads people to repent, we should ask for His extravagant kindness to surround and invade their lives, especially in the midst of their sin.

In the midst of my sin habit of lust, I was bombarded with lies about who I was and whether God still loved me. The deception the enemy was feeding me quickly hardened me to the truth about God's powerful love toward me, resulting in a sick cycle that continued for years. It was only broken by the lavish grace of God evidenced by the Holy Spirit leading me into the truth that eventually set me completely free. You see, God can see who we are created to be because He is the one who fashioned us in our mother's womb. In fact, He never loses sight of our true value and identity, regardless of our behavior. Does God hate sin? Absolutely! But He has this divine ability to see us rightly in the midst of sinful behavior. This is why Romans 5:8 is so powerful. It was in our most sinful state, the place of our deepest shame and regret, that He decided to once and for all proclaim and demonstrate His undying, never failing love for us!

It doesn't say that God demonstrates His love for us when we start walking in a holy manner. His love is demonstrated to us and for us in our weakest, most vulnerable state. This is the heart of God. This revelation is what will take someone who is bound in the deepest and darkest of sins and thrust them into the arms of a loving Savior.

HEAVEN'S CONVERSATION OVER YOUR SIN

> *"My little children, I am writing these things to you so that you may not sin. But if anyone does sin, we have an advocate with the Father, Jesus Christ the righteous." (1 John 2:1)*

As believers we can have no future expectation of sin. John says "if" we sin, not "when." And the beautiful promise that comes if we sin is that there is an advocate right there with us! Not an unholy, sleazy, or lazy advocate trying to get us by with "greasy grace," but Jesus Christ the righteous! Picture this:

You are bound in a sin habit from which you long to be delivered. Day after day and week after week, you continue to struggle, battling the sin from every angle imaginable. After reading books, seeking accountability, and praying desperate prayers you are mentally, emotionally, and physically worn out from the devastating feeling of failure. Every time you fall, there is a genuine sense of remorse paired with a repentant willingness to walk in freedom if only God would crack the door and show you the way out. Well, here is that door...

> JESUS TAKES YOU IN THE MIDST OF YOUR FAILURES THAT YOU'VE NEVER BEEN ABLE TO MASTER, AND HE BECOMES YOUR ADVOCATE BEFORE THE FATHER.

The moment you fall—whatever it is, lust, anger, pride, fear, addiction, you name it—if you are in Christ, I can assure you that Jesus readily desires to present Himself to you as your advocate and helper. He helps you by presenting you to the Father, holy and blameless. That's right, Jesus takes you in your failures that you've never been able to master, and He becomes your advocate before the Father. He starts communicating to the Father on your behalf. Finding freedom from sin habits begins with hearing the conversation that Jesus has with the Father about you. I imagine it went something like this for me:

I am sitting on my bed, hands over my face in disbelief that I fell again. How could I? I was just at church this morning, worshipping the Lord, and just a few hours later I engaged in such a perverted activity. I am such a failure. I'm not the man of God people think I am. I'm not even the kind of man God wants.

As I'm speaking this over myself, hardened in unbelief to the love of God and the reality of what is going on around, Jesus draws close. He sits beside me and places His arm around me. Looking at me, He begins speaking to the Father:

Father, this is your son Peter. Isn't he amazing? Look at how much he loves you and how much he hates his own sin. Remember when he was four years old, and he put his faith in me and was baptized? I washed him in my blood and gave him my own righteousness. We sealed him with the Holy Spirit, and he belongs to us. The only reason he is lusting after women in this way is because our enemy has blinded him from seeing and believing the love we have for him. I love this man as you do, and I am going to keep pursuing him with my love until it consumes him and overwhelms all of his desires. I am going to pursue him until he is free. I am going to pursue him until he experiences an abundant life.

As I began to believe the patient and kind way Jesus advocated to the Father for me, my faith began to rise. *He is for me! He will rescue me! I will be free!* I began to believe that the covenant I had with Jesus was not a disappointment to Him. His confident advocacy for my freedom became a source of strength and joy to me. When we can see that God is fighting *for* us instead of frustrated *with* us, we will maintain the covenant connection that the blood of Jesus purchased. In the midst of a sin struggle, we will remain positioned to receive life and strength from the only One who can set us free.

If you have not had victory in your struggle against sin, I implore you to put your faith in Jesus Christ, an ever-present help in your time of need. It doesn't matter how long you have struggled; He remains your constant Advocate and wonderful Savior. His love will never fail you, but it is only experienced in the realm of faith by God's glorious grace. Faith provides access to what grace provides. Determine in your heart that you will stay in a place of faith, believing in the covenant you have with God that is firmly established by the blood of Jesus. This covenant with God is our only hope of walking in victory. He will not break His covenant with us, even if we sin, because through this covenant we are holy and blameless in Christ.

CHAPTER 15
SEPARATING THE SIN FROM THE SAINT

"For one who has died has been set free from sin."

Romans 6:7

In Romans 6 Paul emphatically establishes the fact that when we were baptized, our old sinful state was buried with Christ, and we came up out of the waters a brand-new creation. In verse 11, he says, "So you also must consider yourselves dead to sin and alive to God in Christ Jesus."

Before I came to understand that the gospel truly liberates us from all the power of sin, I would read Romans 7 and find a strange sense of comfort that someone as revered as Paul also battled sin. Since I struggled repeatedly with looking at pornography, I would read how Paul articulated "doing what he hates" and would be relieved that I was not alone in my sin struggle. However, the more I read Romans and allowed God to renew my mind to the gospel, the more I saw that Romans 7 is not an excuse to keep on sinning but a prescription of how to think as New Testament believers in Christ who are struggling with sin because they are living under the law.

Paul starts by giving an analogy of a man and woman who are married by law. He says that the law of marriage is only in effect as long as both the man and the woman are still alive. If one of them dies, the law of marriage no longer applies to that couple, since one member of the covenant has died. He goes on to define an adulteress as a woman that is seeking intimacy with another man while her husband is still alive. However, if her husband has died, she is free from the law of marriage and is permitted to marry another man.

He uses this analogy to describe our relationship with the law and Jesus. He brings it home by stating that since by faith we have identified with the crucifixion of Jesus, we have in effect died to our former relationship with the law. This means that if we understand the gospel properly, then we will no longer live our lives trying to abide by some spiritual laws in order to merit God's favor. We have died to our prior, legally binding relationship with the law. And the reason we have died to this old relationship is so that we can be free to belong to Jesus, our new Husband.

This belonging to Jesus will ultimately result in us bearing fruit for Him, which is what every Christian longs for. But in order for us to bear fruit, we must first belong to Him, and in order to belong to Him, we must understand, believe, and embrace that we have "died to the law through the Body of Christ" (Rom. 7:4).

A problem in the Church today is that many believers in Christ are married to Jesus but attempt to still have a relationship with the law, their old husband that they are no longer in covenant with. Because they are trying to have a relationship with the law while married to Jesus, they are actually committing adultery with Jesus, and their Christian life is plagued by guilt, shame, and condemnation. The reason they feel so much guilt is because the law reminds them constantly that they are falling short of God's commands. These Christians want to fully and freely belong to Jesus, but they are not comfortable letting their old relationship with the law truly be dead. They fear that if they don't have a list of demands on their life, they will somehow be led astray into sin. However, the only way someone can truly belong to Jesus is if they are completely dead to and set free from a relationship with the law. Paul is teaching the church that the Old Testament laws God gave them (so that they could have a relationship with Him) no longer apply. Why? Because now, through the gospel, they can have full access to intimacy with Jesus because they are made one with Him in His righteousness.

This would make an external law governing a covenant relationship with God useless. As many of us who are married know, a law is pointless in the realm of love. Though I am married to my wife, I do not place laws or demands upon her. A marriage covenant exists and thrives in an environment of grace and love. It is governed completely and entirely by love. It would be senseless to enforce laws within a loving covenant relationship because the very nature of love is that it seeks the desire of the other person. Intimacy in the new covenant is about disclosing desires, not placing demands. If I wish my wife to do something for me or with me, I simply share that desire from my heart, trusting that in her love for me she will be motivated to do that thing. For example, I am always aware of hall or closet lights that are left on. For years I would convey my desire that when we leave the house, I would like for all the lights and fans to be turned off. Though tempted to make a law of this desire, I chose to simply reiterate my desire until at long last it became my wife's desire as well. But to this day she will say that the only reason she turns the closet light off is because she knows it's important to me.

INTIMACY IN THE NEW COVENANT IS ABOUT DISCLOSING DESIRES, NOT PLACING DEMANDS.

But if for some reason she forgets and doesn't fulfill that desire (or some other desire) of my heart, though the desire remains, I must refuse to punish her relationally by withdrawing my affection or love. The temptation is to restate the desire as a command and communicate that there will be relational consequences if that desire is not met. We know we are putting laws on our loved ones when we feel justified in withholding our affection because a certain desire of ours wasn't met. In this way, we place demands and laws upon our loved ones, which contradicts the unconditional nature of the covenant we made in the beginning.

In the same way, God is not placing demands on us to walk righteously. Since He has made us righteous, His communication to us is a disclosure of desire based on our new nature. He asks us to walk in a holy manner because He has given us His Holy Spirit that enables us to do so. The very laws that were external have now been written on our hearts, making righteousness our new nature. Too many Christians try but fail to live holy lives because they are trying to do the right things instead of understanding that they have become the right things. When you understand that you have become the righteousness of God, you will no longer try to do righteous things. You will simply let His nature that He has given you manifest.

So in Romans 7 Paul is giving us a real life example of what it looks like for someone who is still married to the law to try to have a relationship with Jesus. Let's look at this much-debated text:

"What then shall we say? That the law is sin? By no means! Yet if it had not been for the law, I would not have known sin. For I would not have known what it is to covet if the law had not said, 'You shall not covet.' But sin, seizing an opportunity through the commandment, produced in me all kinds of covetousness. *For apart from the law, sin lies dead.* I was once alive apart from the law, but when the commandment came, sin came alive and I died. The very commandment that promised life proved to be death to me. For sin, seizing an opportunity through the commandment, deceived me and through it killed me. So the law is holy, and the commandment is holy and righteous and good. Did that which is good, then, bring death to me? By no means! It was sin, producing death in me through what is good, in order that sin might be shown to be sin, and through the commandment might become sinful beyond measure. For we know that the law is spiritual, but I am of the flesh, sold under sin. For I do not understand my own actions. *For I do not do what I want, but I do the very thing I hate. Now if I do what I do not want, I agree with the law, that it is good. So now it is no longer I who do it, but sin that dwells within me.* For I know that nothing good dwells in me, that is, in my flesh. For I have the desire to do what is right, but not the ability to carry it out. For I do not do the good I want, but the evil I do not want is what I keep on doing. *Now if I do what I do not want, it is no longer I who do it, but sin that dwells within me.*" (Rom. 7:7-20, emphasis added)

So here you have Paul describing the woes of living under the law. I very much believe that he speaking here as a born-again believer who is struggling with being under the law. He acknowledges that the law is in fact good, which is something that is worth stating here. The laws that we seek to follow are often right and good and true and have come from God Himself. However we learn from this text that these laws actually arouse sinfulness within us and cause us to do the very things we hate.

Now let me make a comment here about what I believe Paul is saying in verses 16-17 and reiterating in verse 20. In this text, you see Paul referring to himself in two different ways. He says that there is one part of him that hates the sin that he is doing. But there is another part of him that is doing the very thing that he hates. In verse 17, he says something quite remarkable, which honestly would stir up a lot of criticism and correction if he made this statement in most of today's churches. Look at what he says about the sin he commits: "So now it is no longer I who do it, but sin that dwells within me."

In essence Paul has learned that if he does something sinful, it does not compromise his new God-given nature that was received simply by putting his faith in Jesus. To put it plainly, he is saying, "I (my new nature that I received in Christ) wasn't the one who sinned, it was actually sin dwelling within me that did that." He has clearly established in the previous chapter (Rom. 6) that the one who has identified with the death of Jesus is free from sin (see Rom. 6:7). It is evident that he is giving us language and understanding if we are still battling a sin habit. Paul is essentially saying that it is no longer his new creation that is doing the sin; it is the old sin nature that was put to death, yet that still remains because of the law. Paul teaches us that our old sin nature is dead and has no power over us, unless we resurrect it through trying to live according to the law. If Paul tried to use this language in churches today, I bet many would not appreciate what appears to be a lack of ownership of his sin. We are taught that if we are truly "sorry" for our sin, then we must take ownership of it. But the reality is that it's possible to feel sorry for your sins and still be overcome by them.

JP'S TESTIMONY

JP is one of my best friends to this day, and his testimony illustrates the power of what I'm trying to convey. As a young boy he was abused sexually by various family members, which led him to become confused about his sexuality. As he became a young man, even though he grew up in the church, he started living a life dominated by heterosexual and homosexual immorality. At the height of his pain, he had become a male dancer in a gay club and was contemplating moving to California to start a relationship with another man. Even though JP was a Christian through this whole process and felt sorry for what he was doing, his sorrow and grief were unable to help him find freedom. He was bound to an identity that unbeknownst to him had been crucified and buried with Christ. His past sins and the sins committed against him had deceived JP and hardened his heart to the love of God.

But God's love would not be denied. God intervened miraculously in JP's life. The night before he was going to move, he visited his old life group to tell them his plans and give God one last shot to get ahold of his life. As JP told the group that he identified with the Apostle Paul being imprisoned for his faith, one of the leaders quickly pointed out the difference between JP's life and Paul's. She said, "Paul was imprisoned against his will for sharing the gospel, yet you are sitting a jail cell that has already been opened for you. All you need to do is stand up and leave that cell behind."

She simply gave him permission to be free. By the grace of God, he realized that night that he no longer had to live in bondage and that through a real relationship with Jesus Christ he could be free.

JP came to our church about a month later, having experienced more freedom in his life than ever before. When I saw him, I felt the Lord impress upon me that he was like William Seymour, the old African-American revivalist who started the Azusa Street Revival. Not knowing anything about JP's story, I walked up to him and told him that God views him as a revivalist, like William Seymour, and that God would use him to start revivals through prayer and fasting. God didn't tell me that JP was abused or that he was dancing in male strip clubs months before or that I needed to be careful. Rather, He impressed on me how he sees JP and the destiny that is on his life. JP became one of my best friends. He served as a youth pastor at our church, is married to one of the most amazing women of God, and has two precious daughters. This story of redemption and freedom is only possible through the grace and power of God revealed in the gospel.

HOW TO PRAY WITH A SIN STRUGGLE

Now that Christ has come and was crucified for our sin, we have permission, by the power of His sacrifice, to believe that we are no longer defined by the sinful behaviors we struggle against. So instead of trying to control these sinful behaviors through "doing the right things," we must learn to divorce ourselves from the "sin dwelling in us" through true repentance and pray like this:

Father, I know you forgive me because you have committed to doing so, but I want to come to you and ask for your forgiveness for this thing I have done. I hate this behavior that somehow keeps plaguing me. As a new creation in Christ, your son (or daughter), I despise this sinful behavior and want nothing to do with it. This is destructive and harmful behavior that I was never created for. Because of the cleansing and renewing blood of Jesus, I understand that this sin that manifested in me is not who I really am. Thank you that I have your permission to consider myself dead to it and alive to you! I am no longer a debtor to my flesh (Rom. 8:12) or have any obligation to honor the desires my flesh presents to me. Father, I simply put off this sinful behavior. I declare that I am not a victim of a sinful nature and am no longer prone to wander from you. Holy Spirit, renew my mind and help me to see myself as the Father sees me, even in the wake of my actions. By faith, I choose to put on my new self, which was created after the very likeness of God in true righteousness and holiness (Eph. 4:22-24). In humility, I identify with and receive the godly nature that you have freely given to me by the Holy Spirit.

I am completely dead to the law. Thank you that your affection and blessings don't come to me because I am perfect, but because I have hidden my life in your Son. Thank you, Jesus, for being my advocate to the Father in this moment. Thank you that you do not distance yourself from me or withhold your love because I screw up. According to your Word, you are drawing close to me to help me overcome this sin. Thank you for your patience and willingness to cleanse me completely from unrighteousness. Jesus, I believe that with you, I died to every last one of my sinful desires and that in every way, by the Spirit of God, I am alive to the Father!

If we taught people to pray like this in the midst of their sin struggle, we would see the power and grace of God come into their lives and liberate them completely from all sin. We must access its power daily, because this saving power is how we stand in the gospel.

However, the sad reality is that in many churches, the opposite of this is taught, much less achieved. Christians who struggle with sin are often taught to identify with their brokenness and sin nature. They learn to war against their sinful nature by doing spiritual things instead of leaning into their divine nature. The underlying belief is that the more spiritual discipline you have, the more successful you will be at controlling sinful behavior. What is tricky about this line of thinking is that it is obviously not wrong to practice and cultivate disciplines such as reading the Bible, praying, and fellowshipping with brothers and sisters in Christ. But if the underlying belief and motivation in these activities is that we are somehow gaining a mastery over sin through our discipline, then we have fallen prey to a scheme of the enemy that lures us away from grace. This same problem was happening in the Galatian church and was addressed with some very strong language by the apostle Paul:

> *"But if, in our endeavor to be justified in Christ, we too were found to be sinners, is Christ then a servant of sin? Certainly not! For if I rebuild what I tore down, I prove myself to be a transgressor. For through the law I died to the law, so that I might live to God. I have been crucified with Christ. It is no longer I who live, but Christ who lives in me. And the life I now live in the flesh I live by faith in the Son of God, who loved me and gave Himself for me. I do not nullify the grace of God, for if righteousness were through the law, then Christ died for no purpose." (Gal. 2:17-21)*

Paul asks a troubling question for the believer: if we are walking by faith and seeking to be justified by Christ alone and yet sin, does this mean that Christ advocates sin? He answers with an emphatic "NO!"—any attempt to rebuild the old way of living (through the law) after we have died to it is actually the sin. We prove to be transgressors in that we seek to be justified by the law instead of through Christ alone. Again Paul reiterates in verse 20, "I [the old sinful Paul] have been crucified with Christ and it is no longer I [that sinful man] who lives, but Christ lives in me. And the life I [the new creation Paul] live in this body I [the new creation Paul] live by faith in the Son of God." Paul is again establishing the fact that our old sinful nature is once and for all crucified with Christ. The life we now live as new creations in Christ we live by faith, allowing the Son of God, by the Holy Spirit, to express His life and goodness through us. He goes on to say this in chapter 3:

> *"O foolish Galatians! Who has bewitched you? It was before your eyes that Jesus Christ was publicly portrayed as crucified. Let me ask you only this: Did you receive the Spirit by works of the law or by hearing with faith? Are you so foolish? Having begun by the Spirit, are you now being perfected by the flesh?" (Gal. 3:1-3)*

The Galatian church started off well by hearing the gospel and believing it, which was counted to them as righteousness. However, in just a short time they were tricked into thinking that by their own efforts (the flesh) they could somehow achieve spiritual maturity. They were trying to achieve the righteousness and perfection that the gospel promised to them by adhering to that old Jewish law. Paul rebukes them soundly, with a stern reminder that if they could achieve righteousness through spiritual disciplines (the law), then Christ died for no purpose (Gal. 5:2).

This is very strong language that I believe is very applicable to the Church today. We must stop adding laws and demands on top of the promise of salvation by believing that through our spiritual disciplines we will be made more mature, righteous, or holy. The only way to experience salvation and to mature in our faith is to simply believe. Is this not the gospel we first heard and believed?

GROWING UP IN GOD - STANDING IN RIGHTEOUSNESS

The gospel is often preached as a one-time gift of salvation, but it was never intended to be an isolated experience. We were taught that, no matter what we have done, no matter how dark our sin, if we simply acknowledge our sin, ask for forgiveness, and believe that Jesus Christ paid for all of our sins, then we are forgiven and receive eternal life that will enable us to go to heaven when we die. How beautiful and true this is! But as we have discussed, this is simply the result of our justification, the very first aspect of our salvation!

As we explore the other facets of salvation, namely our sanctification, we will see that this gospel is an all-encompassing message to be leaned upon daily to sustain and mature us into the very likeness of Jesus Himself. Yet, like the Galatians, we have a hard time believing that this message applies to those who have been Christians for some time. We assume that if someone is saved, they would naturally mature in God over time. But the sad reality is that many who have been Christians for years remain babies in Christ. If someone has been a believer for 20 years and is still plagued with the same besetting sins with which they came into the Kingdom, this does not negate the authenticity of their relationship with Christ or their conversion experience. It is only evidence they have not learned to grow up in God.

> THIS GOSPEL IS AN ALL-ENCOMPASSING MESSAGE WE NEED TO LEAN ON DAILY TO BE SUSTAINED AND MATURED INTO THE VERY LIKENESS OF JESUS HIMSELF.

Most of us heard a message that we were able to receive. But we were not taught that the gospel is actually a message to *stand* in and experience daily salvation, as Paul describes:

> *"Now I would remind you, brothers, of the gospel I preached to you, which you received, in which you stand, and by which you are being saved, if you hold fast to the word I preached to you—unless you believed in vain." (1 Cor. 15:1-2)*

Paul wanted to remind the believers of the gospel that he preached. He continually reminded them that this truth is not something to be received once, but an ongoing promise of God's power that will daily rescue and redeem us from all of the effects of sin. This spiritual maturity can only take place by grace through faith:

> *"For by grace you have been saved through faith. And this is not your own doing; it is the gift of God, not a result of works, so that no one may boast." (Eph. 2:8-9)*

This is how we were taught to enter into salvation, and it is how we need to stand in salvation and experience its ongoing power in our lives. It is always by grace through faith:

> *"Therefore, as you received Christ Jesus the Lord, so walk in Him, rooted and built up in Him and established in the faith, just as you were taught, abounding in thanksgiving." (Col. 2:6)*

How did we receive Christ? We received Him by grace and through faith, and it is in this same way that we must learn to walk in Him. The challenge in walking with God by grace through faith is that it takes a continual yielding to the Holy Spirit. I say this is a challenge because most of us are not comfortable simply yielding and believing. We must learn to let God be in control of our walk rather than seeking to control it ourselves. If we trust Him for our entrance into the Kingdom, why do we not trust Him to sustain us in our walk once we become one with Him? Every morning we wake up, we get to listen to the Holy Spirit speak to us through the Word of God and to our hearts.

DON'T LET SIN HARDEN YOUR HEART TO HIS VOICE

The writer of Hebrews warns, "Take care, brothers, lest there be in any of you an evil, unbelieving heart, leading you to fall away from the living God. But exhort one another every day, as long as it is called 'today,' that none of you may be hardened by the deceitfulness of sin. For we have come to share in Christ, if indeed we hold our original confidence firm to the end. As it is said, 'Today, if you hear His voice, do not harden your hearts as in the rebellion.'" (Heb. 3:12-15).

We must not harden our hearts when He speaks to us from His word, by the Holy Spirit, and through others. When we believe what He says, God's grace will be extended to us so that we may experience all the promises of salvation. It is the manner in which we grow up and mature into all God has promised us. We are simply called to believe, to hold fast this message we have heard, not swerving to the right or left, and to allow God to complete the good work He started in us when we first believed.

If we stumble into sin, the deceit that follows combats our belief and confidence, challenging our walk by grace through faith. We have identified this deception as the belief that our sinful behavior indicates a sinful identity. But as we just discussed, we must not allow our hearts to be hardened to the Holy Spirit when He speaks to us, especially if we stumble. We must learn how to stand in the gospel that daily promises to save us from our sin, if we will only have faith that God has crucified our sinful nature and truly made us righteous. As we are established through intimacy in our own journey with God, it will enable and empower us to walk powerfully with those around us who are struggling with sin. In private, as we learn to fight the good fight of faith, refusing to be deceived by sin and persisting in God's grace, we will be well equipped to help other people get back to the gospel and experience true freedom from sin.

CHAPTER 16

DEALING WITH THE SIN OF OTHERS

"Then Peter came up and said to him, "Lord, how often will my brother sin against me, and I forgive him? As many as seven times?" Jesus said to him, "I do not say to you seven times, but seventy-seven times."

Matthew 18:21-22

So how do we practically create an environment of grace for our brothers and sisters who are stuck and truly want freedom from some sin habit? We speak the truth to them in love. We remind them of the New Covenant that they were born into. We appeal to their blood-washed conscience and new identity in Christ. We remind them that righteousness is a gift to be received. We choose kindness and mercy over judgment, believing and hoping that it will lead them to repentance. The Accuser of the Brethren will have a nonstop barrage of terrible things to say about your brothers and sisters in Christ. Operating in grace, we will refuse to agree with the lies and accusations from the enemy about this person that they are broken, fearful, depressed, or perverted. Grace will see them through the eyes of the gospel: "From now on, therefore, we regard no one according to the flesh. Even though we once regarded Christ according to the flesh, we regard Him thus no longer" (2 Cor. 5:16).

If we want to see people set free from sin, we must learn how to extend and exhibit God's grace, so that their God-given righteousness received through the gospel is able to come forth in power. Let me speak to pastors and church leaders specifically for a moment. This is our goal and privilege as shepherds of the flock. We must demonstrate unconditional love to those who are *struggling* with sin and treat them as if they are the most righteous, pure, and holy ones that we've ever met. We must direct them back to the gospel. We must remind and show them how God views them and how valuable they are to His heart. In doing so, we will see the power of sin (the law) broken off of their life, and they will truly be set free from sin's entanglement. We must help them understand that it is *only* by the blood of Jesus that they are made pure and that the only thing they need is faith in this marvelous truth. It is so easy to be deceived into thinking that our failures disqualify us and put us at odds with God. We are confident that God can take a sinner and bring them into the fold, no matter what they've done in their past, but for those of us who have been in God's family for years, we sometimes struggle with thinking that He still loves us in that same unconditional way. We hear the lies that say, *You should know better by now. God has given you so many chances and has been patient with you, but His patience is wearing thin.*

LOVING THEM IN SIN

A common objection I hear from people who want to justify withholding their kindness and affection from people who are stuck or struggling in sin is that they don't want the person to mistake their kindness for approval of their sin. But why would we think that loving someone who is struggling in sin is agreeing with their sin or giving them a license to sin? I have often heard this type of thinking in the Church, and it is so contrary to the gospel. It is human wisdom, a way that seems right to a man but in the end leads to destruction (Prov. 14:12). We think that giving love, affection, and even blessing to someone who is in sin is somehow condoning their sin and empowering them to stay in it. So we punish our Christian brothers or sisters who are in sin by withholding our affection, placing strict demands on them, or warning them of the perils of their behavior.

Again, I am speaking of those who truly long for freedom. Those who want to justify their sinful behavior and are boasting about it should be warned and confronted (Matt. 18, 1 Cor. 5). The way I discern whether or not someone truly wants freedom from sin is a willingness to keep their heart open in relationship and walking in the light with their behavior. Contrastingly, those who are hesitant about walking in the light through confession and who close their heart off to relationship are often stuck and, at least in that moment, unwilling to be shepherded out of their misery. But more often than not, I have encountered believers who are truly broken over their sin and want nothing more than to be completely set free, which is why I have spent significant time addressing this issue.

So if it were true that we needed to punish others or ourselves for sinning, then God really messed up when He sent Jesus to die for us while we were sinning against Him. Why did He do this? Because He wanted us to see how valuable we are to His heart. Paul says that "according to the riches of His grace, which He lavished upon us, in all wisdom and insight" (Eph. 1:7-8), we have been redeemed and forgiven. God thought it was wise to lavish sinners with grace. Do you realize that God was not guaranteed that we would respond to this amazing act of love? The very God we say we follow loved people in the midst of their darkest night to show them that they were made for so much more. But too often we want people to pay for their sins by proving a certain level of repentance. We conclude that if they continue in sin, they are not truly repentant, and we shun them. We lead them to believe that they have chosen this path of rebellion, and we leave them stuck in their sins instead of loving the sin out of them with the gospel of God.

My prayer is that pastors would come back to the gospel and that they would not just preach it to the lost but powerfully demonstrate it to their flocks. When the Church returns to the gospel, we will see the sons and daughters of God arise with robes of righteousness, and old sinful mindsets and habits that we once struggled with will fall away. Any restrictions of man-made religion that have been placed upon our lives will melt like wax, and we will be given Holy Spirit power to destroy the enemies that once plagued us!

LAW IN THE CHURCH

The law was the system of do's and don'ts that governed and determined Israel's relational connection with God and each other. It was a long spiritual list of commands given by God that would allow Israel to have a healthy relationship with Him if they were able to perfectly abide by His regulations. But we know that, because of their sinful nature, Israel was unable to consistently keep the law. Time and time again they transgressed the statutes of God, breaking covenant with the Lord. The law was intended to lead Israel to the realization that they could never actually fulfill the righteousness of the law on their own, so that they would eventually put their hope and faith in a promised Messiah.

Unfortunately, the Church today is filled with similar laws and behavioral regulations that were birthed through religious tradition and false doctrines. Instead of the Church looking like a family where each member has a genuine concern and love for another (remember Jesus said the world would know we are Christians by our love?), we have become a glorified self-help club in many ways. We have countless prescriptions and ministries specifically geared to helping people overcome besetting sins. These ministries have formulated their own way of dealing with or simply managing these sinful behaviors, but they may not provide people with lasting freedom. These ministries present spiritual principles that are often derived from the Scriptures, but that becomes a tightrope that must be walked out perfectly in order to achieve freedom. Those being ministered to are led to believe that if they continue to struggle with sin, then they must not truly be sincere in wanting freedom. In many cases, these believers, battling the power of the sin aroused by these so-called keys to freedom, are condemned, and fellowship is broken. What a tragic cycle, and one that can only be broken by the power of the gospel!

FLOUNDERING FISH - LAW VS. GRACE

To illustrate this tragic cycle, God gave me a picture of what is happening in the body of Christ when believers live under the law and judge others through the lens of the law. It is a sad picture that caused anguish in my soul, but it is helpful for communicating the foolishness of applying the law to the life of a saved believer.

I saw a fish floundering on the banks of a pond gasping for air. Someone walked up to that fish and began to give it instructions on how to swim. You must wiggle your head and body like so, then you will start swimming again. Stop floundering on the banks, you are only losing more air; if you keep doing that, you will surely die.

The picture is very simple. Giving a fish instructions on how to swim is as absurd and useless as giving a true believer instructions on how to walk righteously. The fact that we administer so many rules and regulations for Christians proves that we do not truly believe the gospel. As Paul writes in 1 Timothy 1:9, "We also know that the law is made not for the righteous" (NIV).

> GIVING A FISH INSTRUCTIONS ON HOW TO SWIM IS AS ABSURD AND USELESS AS GIVING A TRUE BELIEVER INSTRUCTIONS ON HOW TO WALK RIGHTEOUSLY.

The law is pointless for the righteous person because the law of God is now written on their heart and woven into their new God-given righteous nature, empowering the believer to naturally live righteously. Just as a fish naturally knows how to swim because it is in their nature, the born-again believer, birthed into God's righteousness, will naturally know how to live righteously by the Holy Spirit that indwells them, counsels them, and leads them into all truth.

There is nothing wrong with ministries deriving spiritual principles from the Word of God and using God's word to encourage and exhort people into freedom. The problem is when we communicate, whether subtly or overtly, that freedom comes based on our ability to fully "obey" or "walk out" these principles.

SETTING PEOPLE FREE

If we truly want to see people set free from their sinful habit, then through the gospel we must first help them see and believe that they are no longer sinners. This is the first step towards freedom. As we have already covered in detail in the previous chapters, sin is deceptive, and the person that is struggling continually with sin is most definitely not believing that God has made them a brand-new creature. We must learn not to view people according to the flesh (what they do), but according to who they have become in Christ (who they are). As Paul writes, "From now on, therefore, we regard no one according to the flesh. Even though we once regarded Christ according to the flesh, we regard Him thus no longer. Therefore, if anyone is in Christ, he is a new creation. The old has passed away; behold, the new has come." (2 Cor. 5:16-17).

As people begin to believe that God's sacrifice truly makes them clean from the inside out and that they are so conflicted and broken over their own sin only because God dwells in them and has given them righteous desires, they will actually feel righteous. The power of sin will begin to wither up and die in their life. This will result in a change in behavior, a change in desire, and ultimately a life changed by the power of God through this glorious gospel!

CHAPTER 17
GLORIFICATION

"Beloved, we are God's children now, and what we will be has not yet appeared; but we know that when He appears we shall be like Him, because we shall see Him as He is. And everyone who thus hopes in Him purifies himself as He is pure."

1 John 3:2-3

When Christ returns in all His glory to establish the everlasting Kingdom of heaven, destroying the powers of darkness by the brightness of His coming, we who have hoped in His return will be glorified in Him by receiving heavenly bodies that will never decay. This final aspect of the triune grace called glorification is God's way of dealing with the presence of sin on the earth and in our physical bodies.

There is little discussion in the Church in regards to the grace of glorification and how it is an integral part of our salvation. John says that the very hope that we have in Christ's return and the full and final manifestation of God's grace produces the purity of Jesus in our life (1 John 3:1-2). Understanding God's heart and purpose in glorifying us will give us an even greater appreciation of this all-encompassing work and help us actually experience the power of this future grace in our lives today.

Remember how the triune work of Christ provides a triune grace that delivers us from a triune problem of sin? The death, burial, and resurrection providing our justification, the resurrected life of Christ providing our sanctification, and His soon coming return providing our glorification. We have seen that justification deals with the penalty of sin, sanctification deals with the power of sin, and, lastly, glorification deals with the presence of sin. We see from the beginning that it took time for sin to fully manifest by killing the human body. James explains the progression of sin in our lives: "But each person is tempted when he is lured and enticed by his own desire. Then desire when it has conceived gives birth to sin, and sin when it is fully grown brings forth death." (Jam. 1:14-15).

BIRTH OF SIN

James explains how sin is birthed in the soul by carnal desires. If we choose to act on those desires, we give birth to sin, and eventually that sin will bring about death in our lives. The glorifying grace of God promised at the second coming will deal with the presence of sin by disarming and dethroning the last enemy of God, which is death. As Paul writes to the Corinthians, "Then comes the end, when He delivers the Kingdom to God the Father after destroying every rule and every authority and power. For He must reign until He has put all His enemies under His feet. The last enemy to be destroyed is death" (1 Cor. 15:24-26).

In light of the atrocities and depravity that fill the headlines in today's news, we have this hope that our King is coming and, with divine justice, will right every wrong and establish His Kingdom forever and ever! This hope is a steady anchor for our soul in the midst of the trials and tribulations that we all face as we enter the Kingdom of heaven (Rev. 1:9, Acts 14:22).

DEATH: GOD'S ENEMY

Since the promise of glorification largely deals with the effect of sin on our mortal bodies, we know that it was never God's desire or design that we should die. Death is clearly defined biblically as an "enemy of God" that will ultimately be defeated at the end of the age (1 Cor. 15:26). Knowing this, we must not accept the belief that death is somehow a tool in the hand of God to instruct or chastise His people. The presence of sin in the earth is most clearly seen through the decay, disease, and death of the physical body. We know that "death [came] through sin" (Rom. 5:12), so we could say that if sin is the tree, then death, disease, and sickness are the fruit of this tree. If we believe that the death, burial, and resurrection of Jesus broke the power of sin (the tree), then we must also believe that death, disease, and sickness (the fruit of that tree) has been disarmed as well.

WE MUST NOT ACCEPT THE BELIEF THAT DEATH IS SOMEHOW A TOOL IN THE HAND OF GOD TO INSTRUCT OR CHASTISE HIS PEOPLE.

The promise of salvation as offered by Jesus Christ does not just touch our spirits or souls but also touches and brings a real deliverance to our mortal bodies. It is for this reason you see one of the primary ministries of Jesus while He walked the earth was healing those who were physically sick, diseased, or afflicted. Many people object to the desire or willingness of God to bring about miracles of divine healing, asking what the point is since we are all going to "die." This demonstrates a lack of understanding of the triune work of Christ and His overwhelming desire of love to thoroughly save mankind.

Romans 8:3 says, "By sending His own Son in the likeness of sinful flesh and for sin, He condemned sin in the flesh." "Sin in the flesh" is sickness, disease, and ultimately death. This does not mean we should conclude that a sinful habit is the reason someone is sick, diseased, or has died. It simply means that, since sin is still in the world, it has and will continue to manifest itself in the flesh of mankind through sickness and disease, and the only remedy for this is the glorifying grace of God promised to His Church. This is why the ministry of Jesus in healing the sick and His exhortation of instruction to all believers to do the same are important mandates from heaven—they demonstrate and reveal His ultimate heart to bring full redemption to the human race. By accepting and receiving this ministry and by recognizing that a partial access to this glorifying grace has been granted to us, we will see that the healing of the sick and raising the dead is simply one more beautiful promise of salvation included in the gospel.

To illustrate that this heavenly reality of health and healing is God's desire for us now, let's look at the prayer that the Lord taught his disciples: "Our Father in heaven, hallowed be your name. *Your Kingdom come, your will be done, on earth* as it is in heaven" (Matt. 6:9-10, emphasis added). In this first part of the Lord's prayer, you have Jesus teaching His disciples, and consequently all believers (Matt. 28:20), that we are allowed and encouraged to pray for two specific things to be done while we are still on this earth. The first thing He encourages them to pray for, connected with the second, is that the Kingdom (or the King's dominion) would come on earth as it is in heaven. The second thing they were encouraged to pray for is the will of God to be done on earth as it is in heaven.

Knowing that in heaven where God's will is always being accomplished, no one is sick, diseased, dying, or dead, we are encouraged to pray that that same reality would come and God's will be done on earth. This is our grounds for praying confidently and boldly that any circumstance we encounter that is contrary to the will of God being done in heaven must give way to the heavenly reality of God's Kingdom and His good, pleasing, and perfect will.

GLORIFICATION

If justification is God's righteousness imparted to our spirit which deals with the penalty of sin (death), and if sanctification is God's righteousness imparted to our soul which deals with the power of sin (law), then glorification is God's righteousness imparted to our bodies that deals with the presence of sin. Though we will not fully experience the glorification of our earthly bodies until Christ returns, I believe that through the gospel we are given access to taste "the powers of the age to come" (Heb. 6:5).

Since glorification is God's power imparting righteousness to our bodies, we know that the ultimate expression and fulfillment of this aspect of salvation will not be complete until the return of Christ. Nevertheless it is fair to believe that God has graciously given us a taste of this glorious power by entrusting to us the ability, by the Holy Spirit, to bring healing and deliverance to those who are afflicted with such calamities. Sickness, disease, and even death itself have given way in this present age at the hands of men and women of God who have believed the word of God and applied its glorious power to those in need. As with the other aspects of our redemption, it is clear that any manifestation of glorification is a work of God and never the result of some human effort. If justification and sanctification are promises to be received by grace through faith, then it is certain that this final aspect of our salvation is obtained in like manner.

THE GOLIATH OF CANCER

Cancer has become a goliath in our day that taunts and terrorizes people with death. Many people assume that, if this giant comes into your life, it will most certainly kill you. It has in fact killed many people, and to date the medical world has not found a suitable cure for this hellish disease. However, I believe that the power of God revealed through the gospel is sufficient for any and every disease that exists on this earth. For this reason, my friend Wade and I regularly pray for people who are on their death beds, regardless of how hopeless the situation may seem.

One summer Wade was called to pray for a man named Jeff, who was surrendered to hospice and given six months to live due to Squamous Cell Carcinoma, an external cancerous tumor under his arm that had grown to the size of a nerf football. The cancer had spread to his lungs, weakened his body, and caused him to lose thirty-five pounds. The chemotherapy he was using had no effect on the cancer as the tumor continued to grow and bleed. But when Wade and his wife Hannah prayed for this man several times over the course of five months, by the glorious grace and power of God, that tumor began to shrink and dissolve. Without any surgery and the power of prayer, Jeff has regained his weight, and every ounce of cancer has been eradicated from his body. This is the power of the gospel and a beautiful example of the glorifying grace of God to bring healing to our physical bodies!

Hopefully, at this point your faith is rising in the greatness of our God and the completeness of His salvation. As the power of God expressed through this gospel begins to overwhelm you, it will be impossible to keep it to yourself! This faith that explodes in your heart from hearing this gospel will produce a host of Kingdom works as you abide in the vine. The growth of these works is a crucial result of the gospel's effect in our hearts, as James argues:

> *"What good is it, my brothers, if someone says he has faith but does not have works? Can that faith save him? If a brother or sister is poorly clothed and lacking in daily food, and one of you says to them, "Go in peace, be warmed and filled," without giving them the things needed for the body, what good is that? So also faith by itself, if it does not have works, is dead." (James 2:14-17)*

LET THE GOSPEL OUT

By receiving the gospel and experiencing the daily power of God saving you from sin in your body, soul, and spirit, you will be prepared as an ambassador for His Kingdom. The gospel is not meant to stay locked up in our hearts only for us to enjoy. It is also not intended to be locked within the four walls of the church for a select few "chosen" ones to enjoy. It is meant to be proclaimed to the whole world.

I thank God for the evangelists who have paved the way of the gospel message and seen thousands and millions come to Christ through their efforts. I also thank God for the missionaries and evangelists whom we've never heard of, who one by one win souls for Christ. We will have a mighty celebration in heaven with all the great men and women of faith that have gone before us. And, because we have such a great cloud of witnesses who have left us a legacy of love, selflessness, and devotion, it is my desire to ignite that same passion in the Church at large.

I want to start a fire in the hearts of each and every believer reading this book, so that this gospel, which perhaps you were once numb to, comes alive in your spirit and gives you a heart to reach the lost with this good news. And I want to encourage you that you have a significant role to play in reaching the lost. Evangelism is not what many people have made it out to be. It is not only for a few chosen ones. It is the work of the entire Church. As we are rooted and grounded in the love of our Father, we will learn how to partner with God to see

His lost sons and daughters come home.

> *"For the Son of Man came to seek and to save the lost." (Luke 19:10)*

> *"Jesus said to them again, "Peace be with you. As the Father has sent me, even so I am sending you." (John 20:21)*

One of the biggest challenges the Church is facing in this hour is that her expression in the world no longer seems to be relevant. She is often limping along, building bigger walls, putting her hopes in the kingdoms of this world (businesses, retirement, politics), and insulating herself from the "big bad world." Many times, she bemoans the moral decline and corruption in society, while failing to acknowledge her role and position as the "light of the world." A victim mentality has invaded the hearts and minds of many believers, which leads to a spirit of fear, complaining, and eventually apathy. We have forgotten our ancient roots, or better yet we have forgotten our Head, who is Jesus Christ. We have lost touch with the One who came to seek and save the lost. We have become disjointed, and only as we get back to the gospel will we be reminded that, if the world is getting darker, it is only because we have failed to go into it and shine.

The remaining chapters of this book will seek to encourage you, prod you, and compel you to become reunited with the heart of God for the lost. One of the saddest realities in our day is that churches have become focused on building their own kingdoms instead of seeking the Kingdom of heaven first. When we seek the Kingdom, we realize that there are countless millions around us oppressed by the enemy and perishing without having put their faith in Jesus Christ.

THE GOSPEL TO THE LOST?

Knowing now that our salvation is not only a one-time event but an ongoing experience and promise of freedom through intimacy with Jesus, many people will wonder how then to communicate this gospel to the lost and subsequently how to walk with them in such a way that they grow up into that salvation. Paul, knowing the entrance and doorway into the Kingdom of heaven (Christ, and Him crucified) chose to focus his message for the lost on the work of the cross (1 Cor. 2:2-4). In addition to this, he demonstrated the power of God by the Holy Spirit, so that the hearers would not be tempted to put their faith in the intellect or wisdom of Paul but instead trust entirely in God's power to save them. When we take this gospel to the lost, it would be wise to take a similar approach as Paul, preaching Christ and Him crucified and demonstrating the power of the Holy Spirit.

CHRIST CRUCIFIED

We have devoted a large portion of this book in explaining the work of Christ and how through His all-sufficient work we have access by faith into this grace, in which we now stand. So we will not revisit the details. Instead, we will focus on the importance of leading people to the cross. The Son of Man hanging on a cross for the sins of mankind is the greatest and most compelling act of love that this world has ever seen. It cannot be matched! There is power, wonder-working power, in this precious blood of Jesus. It rescues the dying from the throes of hell, washes them clean, and thrusts them from an old cursed heritage of sin and brokenness into the family of God. The lost will never understand the blessings and joy of being in a new covenant with God without first repenting of their sin and receiving the work of the cross.

THE SON OF MAN HANGING ON A CROSS FOR THE SINS OF MANKIND IS THE GREATEST AND MOST COMPELLING ACT OF LOVE THAT THIS WORLD HAS EVER SEEN.

I believe this is why so many churches and evangelists have rightly chosen to focus on this foundational aspect of the gospel. In one sense, as much as this book has been about exploring and rediscovering the fullness of the gospel, it is true that the most important aspect of our salvation is simply putting our faith in Christ for the forgiveness and removal of our sins. This results in our spirits being saved from the penalty of death ensuring us, from the deposit of the Holy Spirit, that we will indeed live forever with our Lord in heaven. What a glorious promise and hope we have in Him! It is not only our privilege to preach this gospel, but we fulfill our ministry by allowing His divine love to flow through us in power!

> *"For I will not venture to speak of anything except what Christ has accomplished through me to bring the Gentiles to obedience—by word and deed, by the power of signs and wonders, by the power of the Spirit of God—so that from Jerusalem and all the way around to Illyricum I have fulfilled the ministry of the gospel of Christ." (Rom 15:18-19)*

CHAPTER 18

DEMONSTRATING LOVE

"Do not imprison Christ in you. Let Him live, let Him manifest Himself, let Him find vent through you."

John G. Lake

The Bible teaches us that no one has ever seen God, but the Son, Jesus Christ, has made Him known. This means that if we want to know God and find out what He is like, we must start by looking at the life of Jesus! The apostle John describes God in the simplest of terms: "God is love." He doesn't say God is loving or that God knows how to love. He says emphatically that God is love. This means that the very essence and nature of His being is love. He then goes on to reiterate the fact that no one has seen God, but if we actually love one another, then we display palpable evidence that God lives in us.

The gospel takes ordinary people, who were previously cut off from experiencing intimacy with God, and makes us so clean that God is literally able to come and make His home inside us. Without the cleansing blood of Jesus, it would be impossible to be made one with God. But now God has poured His love into our hearts by the Holy Spirit. As we understand this beautiful reality and begin to enjoy fellowship and intimacy with God, we will begin to look like Him. His patience becomes our patience. His kindness will shine through our eyes. His power will be released as we lay hands on the sick. His holy authority will rest upon the words that we speak because He lives inside of us. Perfect love has now made His home in our hearts, delivering us from any fear of man and empowering us to actually love others.

This is the gospel, the power of God. This deep connection with God is what will ultimately cause us to effortlessly bear the radical Kingdom fruit that we have been longing for. Common sense and logic tells us that trees do not have to try to bear fruit. Trees simply send their roots down deep, absorb the water, and rest in the sun. Given the right elements, God's design will take over, and fruit will grow. It is the same with the Christian. We must first hear and understand the gospel and allow the roots of our heart to bury deep into the heart of God through fellowship with Him, and the result will be rivers of living water flowing from our lives.

I know for many of you this sounds good, but you might still be wondering what it looks like to bear Kingdom fruit without "striving." The thought of sharing your faith, praying for the sick, or approaching strangers is scary because we have been taught that success hinges on how people respond. But our success is not in how people respond; it is in whether or not we actually manifest love.

One of the ways the Bible defines love is that love does not demand its own way. This means that we don't have to demand that people respond to what we share or do in love. If we know that God lives in us and if we are confident that we have something to give, then we don't have to worry about what people do with what we give them. Our job is to be faithful messengers, giving away what we have freely received. What is it that we are giving? Simply put, we are giving away love. We are giving away God in us, which is the Holy Spirit.

I often train believers to go out on the streets to help them grow in their understanding of what it means to simply love people. Many people are afraid at first, until I help renew their mind to what is actually happening when they share God's love with others. I give them each a $5 bill and tell them that their first job is to find anyone to simply hand the money to and walk away. They don't have to say anything if they don't want to. Now when I ask people if they are scared to do that, no one seems to have a problem! They actually get excited, because they know that when they simply bless a random stranger with money, the stranger, regardless of where they stand with God, will be grateful for the kind gesture.

This is the heart of the gospel. We have freely received the gift of God, the Holy Spirit, and it is now our pleasure and joy to go into the world and freely give what we've freely received. Since the true ministry of reconciliation is so much more valuable than money, I want to give some practical examples of what it looks like to give away the love of God to others. Romans 2:4 says God's kindness leads men to repentance. As we manifest the loving kindness of God to others, they have an encounter with the living God, their Creator. We can trust that, as He encounters the lost through us, He is also drawing men unto Himself. He draws them into repentance and salvation as we demonstrate His love and kindness!

DEMONSTRATING THE GOSPEL

Representing God to the world is not for a select few super Christians; it's the ministry of every believer to manifest the heart of God. This will be an automatic byproduct of cultivating intimacy with Him. And, as we have already established, our intimacy with God starts and ends with His great love for us. It is actually possible to walk in Kingdom power without the love of the King, but the Bible teaches us that any Kingdom activity that is not done in love is pointless.

When Jesus sent His disciples into the world, He instructed them to proclaim the gospel and to heal the sick, raise the dead, cleanse the lepers, and cast out demons. These acts of powerful love let people know that God's Kingdom had come near, calling them to change the way they were thinking. The gospels are full of countless stories of Jesus and the disciples ministering to people without placing demands upon them. Jesus would raise the dead and then go on His way. He would heal the sick and then feed them for hanging around so long! He did not tell the woman with the issue of blood that she must now go to the synagogue every Sabbath. He did not ask her to pray a prayer. He did not tell her to bow down and worship Him. He told the woman, "Go in peace." What do you think she did? With her newfound health and life, that woman was filled with love for Jesus. She became obsessed with Him in such a way that she left everything and began to follow Him. In a moment, Jesus rescued her from 13 years of agony and gave her the freedom to go and live her life.

This kind of unconditional, powerful, and liberating love is irresistible. And it is this exact type of love that we are called to demonstrate. The Church is in desperate need of a reformation, not only in theology but in love. If we are honest, many of our hearts have become dull and numb to the hurting and dying. We may have forgotten how to seek and save those who are lost. We've forgotten that we have what the world needs. We are not lacking anything we need for this work, as many may feel; we have been given everything we need for life, and life abundant! We have been born of God, filled with the Holy Spirit, and empowered to love our neighbor with the exact same transformational love that we have received.

> THE CHURCH IS IN DESPERATE NEED OF A REFORMATION, NOT ONLY IN THEOLOGY BUT IN LOVE.

THE FIRST HEALING

When I came to this idea that God desired to use me to bring physical healing to someone's life, I was living and playing professional soccer in Mikkeli, Finland. I finally mustered the courage to go and find someone who would allow me to pray for them to be healed. I decided to go down to my favorite pizza place to look for someone there, and, in case I didn't find anyone, I could grab some lunch. While I was eating some pizza, a young man hobbled in on crutches with a sports wrap on his ankle. My heart began to pound just thinking about approaching this guy and his girlfriend. Not wanting to distract them from lunch, I waited about 30 minutes until they were done eating. As they exited the restaurant, I was waiting for them with an awkward smile and as much faith in my heart as I could muster. Avoiding any small talk, I cut right to the chase, "Hey, would you mind if I prayed for your ankle to be healed? I believe God can take the pain away and heal whatever is wrong." The young man resisted saying, "No, it's fine. It won't work." I persisted one more time, and apparently his girlfriend felt sorry for me so she said, "Fine, you can try."

I knelt down, placed my hand on his ankle, and prayed a simple prayer. Something like this, "Jesus, I ask that you would heal this ankle, take away all the pain, and make it feel brand-new." I stood, still feeling the adrenaline in my body from taking this step of faith, and asked if he could put weight on it. As he took his weight off the crutches and stepped down on his foot, he exclaimed an expletive in Finnish that I'd rather not repeat. Now the three of us, completely shocked that it worked, began to laugh and rejoice at the goodness of God.

I shared with this couple that it was only by the power and name of Jesus that he had been healed and that Jesus loved them both and wanted to have a relationship with them. They thanked me, then the young man whose ankle had been healed gave his crutches to his girlfriend and began to walk away perfectly, without any pain!

THE BODY OF CHRIST

One of my favorite things about the Body of Christ is how diverse this expression of love can be. We should not expect every Christian to express their faith and give love in the same way. Look at what Paul says about the diversity of the Body:

"For the body does not consist of one member but of many. If the foot should say, 'Because I am not a hand, I do not belong to the body,' that would not make it any less a part of the body. And if the ear should say, 'Because I am not an eye, I do not belong to the body,' that would not make it any less a part of the body. If the whole body were an eye, where would be the sense of hearing? If the whole body were an ear, where would be the sense of smell? But as it is, God arranged the members in the body, each one of them, as he chose. If all were a single member, where would the body be? As it is, there are many parts, yet one body." (1 Cor. 12:14-20)

God is so vast in His love and ways that it is necessary to imitate Him in various ways, uniquely expressed through each of His children. I often try to help people understand what this looks like practically for them, and I will do the same for you. You see, it is the most natural thing for children to imitate their parents. In the most basic way, this is how all kids grow up. They grow up by watching the world around them and learning how to do things by observing the people older and more mature than them. This obviously takes place most frequently in the home. But not every child can perfectly imitate their dad or mom. To each child, there are certain things that will stick out and become natural to imitate. It may be a mannerism, facial expression, or phrase they pick up on just by being around them. In the same way, every born-again believer who cultivates fellowship with God is able to manifest the nature of God by the power of God's Spirit dwelling in their hearts by faith. The nature of God is given to us uniquely, and each member of the Body of Christ has the ability to imitate an aspect of God in a way that no one else can. This is the beauty and the power of the Body of Christ.

I have always been drawn to God's power to save and to heal. I love the stories in the Old Testament where God stretches out His mighty hand and delivers Israel from the Egyptians or when Elijah calls down fire on Mt. Carmel. These stories thrill my soul, and something inside of me longs to see God move in this way. For this reason, I feel one of the areas where I get to imitate God is as a healer and deliverer. I love praying for the sick or for those who are oppressed by the enemy. Something inside of me loves to laugh at and mock the devil, because I know that is what God is like. The Bible says He scoffs at His enemies and makes sport of them. Too many Christians are afraid of the devil and his schemes because they don't understand how powerful they are as children of God. So one of the things I get to imitate is God's strength and zeal for those who are in bondage.

But my wife is so different than me. She is perhaps the most compassionate person I have ever met. She can read a story about an injustice being done to an orphan, and her heart will break. She can instantly start shedding tears for someone she has never met. She loves reading about the redemption stories in the Bible where Jesus stops and ministers to the one individual. So my wife has the ability to imitate an aspect of God that is so completely different and unique than what God has put in my heart, but both are used by God to bring people into His Kingdom.

If you can discover the aspect of God that most excites you or causes you to fall in love with God, that is most likely the aspect of God's heart that He has woven into you and that you will most naturally imitate. If God reveals Himself to us as a provider, He will then allow us to experience that part of His heart by actually providing for others in supernatural ways through us. If we come to know God intimately as a provider, then He will invite us to actually represent His nature as a provider to the world around us. This is the way the world is going to be reconciled back to God.

> THE ASPECT OF GOD THAT MOST EXCITES YOU OR CAUSES YOU TO FALL IN LOVE WITH GOD IS MOST LIKELY THE ASPECT OF HIS HEART THAT HE HAS WOVEN INTO YOU FOR YOU TO NATURALLY IMITATE.

Through the gospel, we all become ambassadors of Christ, reconciling the world back to God first and foremost by not counting their sins against them and then by demonstrating His love through allowing His Spirit to manifest through us. So instead of making evangelism only a message we preach, it becomes a life of love, showing people what God is like. We give to the world abundant life because that is what we have in Christ. It is in giving to the world that our message and ministry will come with power and authority. It was the same in Jesus' day. Jesus would teach, but then He would demonstrate His love through forgiveness, healing, and deliverance. The people were amazed because His teaching actually came with a demonstration of power. Jesus wasn't just telling people about the goodness of God—He was showing it to them. And if we want to see the gospel advance in power wherever we are, we must be willing to imitate God, to walk in love, and to freely give what has been given to us.

CHAPTER 19

BEING CHRISTIAN VS. DOING CHRISTIAN

"Therefore be imitators of God, as beloved children. And walk in love, as Christ loved us and gave himself up for us, a fragrant offering and sacrifice to God."

Ephesians 5:1-2

God reveals Himself *to* man in order for Himself dwell *in* man so that He can manifest Himself *through* man. God's purpose in saving us is first and foremost to be intimate with us. The outcome of intimacy with Jesus is becoming more like Him and loving what He loves. The best way to grow in His image and love for others is to imitate Him. And the best way to be fashioned into His image and likeness is by resting in the grace and acceptance of God.

There are so many Christians trying to do the right "Christian" things and constantly feeling as though they are failing. They compare themselves with other people in ministry and begin to judge their own fruit compared to others. Feelings of inadequacy drive them harder and harder into a cycle of dead works. But the beauty of God's promise of salvation is that we get the privilege of actually becoming like the Lord. When we allow our Father to shape and mold us with His powerful hand of love, we will become like the Son, and our entire life will be filled with Kingdom fruit without us having to try.

One afternoon, as I was riding the train home from work, I watched a public transport officer issue a young girl a citation for not having a ticket for the train. She was devastated and began crying, telling the officer that she had no money to pay the fine and that her parents were going to be very upset with her. She was begging for mercy to no avail. I immediately had the thought that, because Jesus paid my debts, I can offer to pay for hers. It could serve as a testimony to both the officer and the young girl.

Though I only had about $30 in my wallet, I walked up to her and simply said, "Jesus wants you to know that He pays all of your debts and He loves you very much." I turned to the officer and said, "And He has paid all of your debts as well and loves you very much." And then I paid her ticket and walked away. I simply felt led to imitate the kindness and generosity of Jesus in hopes that, after that encounter, the young girl and the officer would have a clearer picture of what Jesus is like.

WE'VE MADE CHRISTIAN MINISTRY MORE ABOUT THE MESSAGE WE PREACH THAN THE LIFE WE LIVE.

Because we have failed to believe and embrace the new nature we've been given, we have quite tragically made evangelism about "works." We have copied and emulated models and strategies of evangelism seeking the latest techniques that will make the gospel "relevant" to the world that has all but written the Church off as archaic and narrow minded. We've made Christian ministry more about the message we preach than the life we live. I remember that, as God was renewing my mind to this reality, I asked Him a simple question. "God, how did you do evangelism?" He led me to the most famous evangelistic passage:

> *"For God so loved the world, that he gave his only Son, that whoever believes in him should not perish but have eternal life. For God did not send his Son into the world to condemn the world, but in order that the world might be saved through him." (John 3:16-17)*

Then He told me something very peculiar that has forever changed my mind about evangelism. I heard Him say, "I never preached that verse; I lived it."

> *"For God so loved the world that He gave…"*

Let's stop right there for a moment and meditate on this. The world was in the height of its rebellion against God and His laws, yet God was overcome by love for His children that had turned against Him. His love was so intense for us that He gave us something of indescribable worth. He gave us Himself. When God wanted to "evangelize" the world, He was compelled by love to give us heaven's best. I wonder if we would see more people "saved" if we genuinely allowed His love to overtake our hearts? How would the Kingdom of God grow on earth if we began to demonstrate His generous love by extravagantly giving from all we have received from God, rather than just telling people an extravagant love exists?

The Church, as the Bride of Christ, has the power, wisdom, resources, love, and freedom that the world needs. God has put within His Church the answer to all the world's problems. But some have been influenced by this world to subtly move from a heart of love and make evangelism into a quantifiable ministry metric. They have succumbed to the temptation to measure their success and compare it to other people and other ministries.

The result is a "gospel" that is shared out of a false motive to achieve a testimony or result instead of from a heart of love and compassion to see someone truly reconciled to their Father. There is nothing wrong with having people pray and acknowledge God as their Savior, and this is a powerful way of verbally expressing our belief in God. But if ministries are using these things as the only measuring rod of success, then I think we have missed something.

When Jesus died, He did not have much to show for it. Seemingly three years of ministry went down the tubes in one giant scandal and disappointment. If we look at the life and ministry of Jesus through the lens and metrics used in most ministries today, we would conclude His ministry was nothing more than a flash in the pan. His methods and humility didn't make sense. His death especially didn't add up to those who were expecting a King to establish a Kingdom. Even those closest to Him were confused and heart broken. You see, Jesus didn't shout from the cross with His dying breath, "Believe in me, or you will die in your sins!" What did He say? "Father forgive them, for they know not what they do." (Luke 23:34) He placed no demand on them because "love does not demand its own way" (1 Cor. 13:5). Love (even though it is right!) does not demand its own way.

Another example of this love is in the garden of Gethsemane right before Jesus is arrested. Let's take a look at one of Jesus' evangelism techniques:

> *"And when those who were around Him saw what would follow, they said, 'Lord, shall we strike with the sword?' And one of them struck the servant of the high priest and cut off his right ear. But Jesus said, 'No more of this!' And He touched his ear and healed him." (Luke 22:49-51)*

Here Jesus is approached by a group of men that are going to arrest Him and lead Him to His death. We might call people like this "enemies" in our day. So as Malchus the high priest's servant approached Jesus to arrest Him, Peter takes out a sword and cuts off his ear. Unfortunately for Malchus, Peter was not in ministry mode, because he was still thinking of protecting what he had instead of seeing the opportunity at hand. In this day and age, we would commend Peter's boldness and would malign Malchus for being on the wrong side of the table. But strangely, in this account, the opposite happens. Jesus turns to Peter, rebukes him, and in one touch puts Malchus' ear back on. We do not find that Jesus says anything to Malchus when He healed his ear in any of the biblical accounts of this story.

Yet undoubtedly if this happened in our day and Jesus was sharing this testimony at one of our church services, He would be asked, "Jesus, did you share the gospel with Malchus? You didn't just heal his ear and not tell him the gospel did you?" My prayer for you is that God would give you a new perspective and strategy for seeing people reconciled back into the family of God. May we adopt the strategy of the Lord, which is simple, extravagant love empowered by the Holy Spirit Himself.

For God so loved the world He gave....

Jesus so loved Malchus He gave him his ear back.

Jesus so loved blind Bartimaeus He gave him his vision back.

Jesus so loved Jairus He gave him his daughter back.

Jesus so loved us He gave us His life so we could have everlasting life.

Do you see the pattern? Jesus loved people so He gave them what everyone is looking for—abundant life. Everywhere Jesus went, He encountered people whose lives had been dominated by the works of the devil, and, with one word, one touch, or one smile, He destroyed those works and gave them life. This is the gospel! This is the Kingdom of God that is at hand!

CHAPTER 20

MINISTRY OF RECONCILIATION

"All this is from God, who through Christ reconciled us to himself and gave us the ministry of reconciliation; that is, in Christ God was reconciling the world to himself, not counting their trespasses against them, and entrusting to us the message of reconciliation. Therefore we are ambassadors for Christ, God making his appeal through us. We implore you on behalf of Christ, be reconciled to God. For our sake he made him to be sin who knew no sin, so that in him we might become the righteousness of God."

2 Corinthians 5:18-21

There are countless ministries out there, but there is one ministry that every born-again believer has been given, and it is this one primary ministry that I want to focus on.

It is called the ministry of reconciliation. God makes His appeal through us: "Be reconciled to God!" We have become ambassadors for Christ, representing the heart of God to mankind. This is the highest honor, privilege, and calling for the Body of Christ. This means we have His delegated authority to represent His nature, His will, and His heart at any time of any day. Representing Him to the world around you by what you say and do is the ministry of reconciliation. God now lives in us (His Body) by the Holy Spirit, and through us He demonstrates the fact that Jesus is alive and continues to seek and save those that are lost. Before we as Christians ever endeavor to build our own ministries, we should first understand the ministry God has already given us and seek to steward it in a way that honors Him. And to be abundantly clear, any ability or competency we have as ministers of this New Covenant comes to us from God, so that no one can boast:

> *"Not that we are sufficient in ourselves to claim anything as coming from us, but our sufficiency is from God, who has made us sufficient to be ministers of a new covenant, not of the letter but of the Spirit. For the letter kills, but the Spirit gives life." (2 Cor. 3:5-6)*

I believe "ministry of reconciliation" and "evangelism" can be used interchangeably. In fact I think it might be more helpful to use the phrase "ministry of reconciliation," because as we have seen the term evangelism has become unclear to many people. When I ask people what they think of when they hear the word "evangelism," the responses include handing out tracts, door-to-door ministry, crusades, salesmen of the church, and so on. I believe the reason evangelism has been relegated to a handful of outgoing, sincere believers is because we've reduced the gospel's "success" to how someone responds to a message or invitation.

MEASURING SUCCESS

I have spent a lot of time on the streets sharing my faith with people. Early on I struggled greatly, because I thought that my success was directly linked with how many people responded positively to what I was saying or doing. I subconsciously needed a response from people to feel successful. If we are honest, some of our ministries demand a response from people so that success can be measured. The problem with this type of demand is that it moves our ministry out of the realm of love and into the realm of human wisdom.

When we approach a stranger with a false motive, it becomes instantly obvious, the encounter is cut short, and the person to whom we tried to speak with is no closer to God than before. However if we approach people in love, knowing that we ourselves have been born again, filled with the Spirit, and have life to give, we will become fountains of blessing to others. When we become a living, breathing manifestation of love, people will have an authentic opportunity to encounter the living God. A true encounter with Him leads to an invitation to be reconciled to Him.

I don't believe the ministry of reconciliation is for a select few Christians who have the right personality. Evangelism is not a sales pitch. It is not something just for outgoing people. Evangelism is simply reconciling the world to God through the proclamation and demonstration of the love of God. When people see, hear, and encounter God through our lives they are changed forever. We reconcile people to God by becoming a living, breathing manifestation of Jesus Christ wherever we go.

EVANGELISM IS RECONCILING THE WORLD TO GOD THROUGH PROCLAIMING AND DEMONSTRATING THE LOVE OF GOD.

THE NEW BREED

"Look carefully then how you walk, not as unwise but as wise, making the best use of the time, because the days are evil" (Eph. 5:16). It is high time the pure and spotless Bride of the Lamb awake from her slumber, for the glory of the Lord has risen upon her and the dying world is desperate to know this King of Glory!

Our Father is the greatest evangelist the world has ever known. He so loved the world that He gave His Son! It is through His act of love that men and women are forever forgiven of their sins and reconciled into His family. God is raising up a generation of believers who understand that the gospel does not start with the separation of man from God, but instead with God's desire to bring man back into the eternal covenant of the Godhead. These believers will lay their own lives down to show the length, breadth, and height of God's love to those stuck in sin and death, who are not yet in God's family. These ones will not simply talk about the love of God, but they will violently insert themselves into the chaos that consumes the lost with a light and love so brilliant that the powers of darkness will tremble. They will give their time, their resources, and their very lives to see people encounter the love of the Father that has laid hold of them through the life of Jesus. Now is the time for sons and daughters of God to be revealed, who will not only preach this glorious gospel but will radically live it.

These people are a new breed rising up on the earth today. They are simple people who will change the world one day and one person at a time. They are a people possessed by love. They are free from fear. They are bold. They are kind. They are patient. They are powerful. They are humble, and they are joyful. They associate with the poor and dine with kings. Wherever they go, they start revivals...or riots. They are often mistaken for angels or gods. They are a holy people. They are righteous. They are unusual. They move and blow like the wind. They are feared, and they are loved, and they are hated all at the same time. They are often misunderstood. They are neither puffed up by the praises of man nor torn down by their criticism. How can they be? They know they are loved. They are ordinary people who have been possessed by an extraordinary God. They look like God. They act like God. They love like God. They are born of God. They are filled with God.

These people are called Christians. They hear the gospel, believe it, and are transformed by it. They are born again into an intimate love affair with the living God, and nothing can shake their confidence in Him. They are not bold in their own right or because they have tried hard. They are not the superstars of the Christian world. They are simply those who believe. They are childlike. They hear the voice of God, submit to it, and as a result become a unique race of people. They are God's literal body on the earth, carrying out His revealed will wherever they go by the power of the Holy Spirit.

They are in love, and it is obvious. It's the thing that motivates them. They are compelled by love. They are free from seeking their own desires. They live to see people set free into the same love affair they enjoy. Their joy is contagious. Their laughter sets people free from addiction and self-hate. They seek the lost. They go after the one. They pursue the most hopeless situations, because they know love never fails. They raise the dead. They cast out devils. They heal the sick. They speak with authority. They are set free from sin. It shows on their face, because they have forgotten what shame feels like. They radiate God's glory. They reflect His goodness. They demonstrate His kindness. They share their food with the poor. They give without sparing. They never lack. They are God's kids, and the world knows it.

The earth groans and cries out to see this breed rise up. The entire world is longing for it. The devil is trying to stop it, for if he had known this would happen, he would have never crucified the Lord of Glory. Now, instead of one God-man, there are many sons of glory. The revealed sons of God are able to destroy the works of the devil and establish the Kingdom of heaven on earth through powerful acts of love! Sin, sickness, and death all give way at their command. These are the children of God, the Bride of Christ that are covering the earth in these last days.

B

Braveheart

Braveheart Ministries, Inc. exists to equip the Church for works of ministry, to proclaim the gospel of the Kingdom, to heal the sick, and to pray that God would continue to send laborers into the harvest.

Learn more at **braveheartministries.org/**

Made in the USA
Las Vegas, NV
19 October 2024